Now What?

AN NCO'S GUIDE TO SUCCESS

By Harrison Burkardt

Foreword By Bob Vasquez, Cmsgt (Ret), Usaf

ISBN 978-1667813462

To all of those who have given me the opportunity to be a part of their lives,

to the Airmen, who have allowed me to help them grow.

To those Airmen, you have taught me how to become a better NCO.

Contents

Foreword by Bob Vasquez, CMSgt (Ret), USAF

❧

The essence of success is not getting or having, it's giving and helping. Within the pages of this book, Harrison Burkardt shares his thoughts, perspectives, musings, and experiences on what it takes to be a successful Noncommissioned Officer (NCO) in today's Air Force. He keys in on many topics that are essential to succeeding as a leader in the military and civilian worlds. To note, he mentions that "People stay at their job because they love the people they work with." This is true whether you're a leader or a follower. The success of any organization is created and maintained by the relationships the members of the organization develop and maintain. It's often called culture. A culture, in its most basic form, is based on what people do. What Harrison shares here is what he believes an NCO, especially an effective one, does on a daily basis to create a culture where everyone thrives.

One of the areas of professional development that's not addressed often enough is peer leadership. This book is all about peer leadership. It's written as a peer sharing thoughts and methods to those who are about to experience having to lead others of similar rank and experience as well as those more junior to them. Leading peers is not easy. But Harrison's book will help you consider what you might want to work on. One of my favorite truisms is, "To know but not to do is not to know." Every chapter includes questions and challenges that will encourage you to take some action. Don't just do it. Do it now. Do it right. And make it last.

ALL IN! ALL THE TIME!

bob vásquez!

Bob Vásquez, CMSgt (Ret), USAF

Introduction

Wat in Mother Martha's sweet green Earth could a TSgt know about being a successful NCO? I'm still living and breathing it, as are you! We've communicated daily. We've shared stories. I've learned from you, as I hope you can learn from me. Allow me to guide you on the principles I believe make for a successful NCO.

Over the course of this book, we will lay the foundation, but you will have to pave your own unique road. It took me quite some time to find what I truly loved (twenty-nine years, to be exact). Eight years of my Air Force career was on autopilot as a SrA until I was sent to be a member of the Base Honor Guard. My first thought was, 'Why the hell would they send an eight-year SrA to Honor Guard?' I thought being a member of the Honor Guard was a reward for stellar performers. They took a shot on me. The experience at Honor Guard was life-changing. I felt as if I was a part of a team, a part of something bigger than myself. Working with NCO's who were still in their first enlistment was inspiring. My six months flew by. Returning to my primary duty, dental assisting, was quite the challenge initially. I told myself it was different. People weren't the same. I believed it was everyone's problem but mine. I created the issue. I allowed my mind to become the culture.

A spot for the Base Honor Guard NCOIC position became available. The first year I applied, I was denied, but the following year, I submitted again and was approved for the role. This was my first taste of leadership in my then nine-year career. There were about eighteen to twenty Airmen spanning across all different AFSCs to provide guidance and training for. I had zero troops prior. I also had no real leadership role or responsibility. The Airmen of the 355th DMAFB Honor Guard humbled me with the opportunity to lead. My boss (who was never really a boss) allowed me free range to roam and expand my leadership toolkit. Now, I say he was never really a boss because he wasn't very orthodox.

On my first day on the job, he invited me to a Mac Demarco concert. I didn't know who the guy was, but I went. The extent of my year term at Honor Guard as the NCOIC was extremely unorthodox, in the best way possible. The feeling of rank was never there. All I ever felt there was care and support. Trust was always there. Teamwork was a must. Communication came easy. My boss quickly became a brother, which translated to amplifying my care and support to those eighteen to twenty Airmen. It took someone else showing me I could be a leader to wake up, and five attempts to make SSgt. After Honor Guard, it took one attempt to make TSgt.

I went back to my primary duty with a totally different attitude. No one would take it from me. I was empowered to teach the art of leadership to anyone willing to listen. It was my choice now, no one else's. Hopefully, this helps you find your true calling quicker than I did. A lot of the experiences shared, I've seen firsthand. Like a hawk, I've watched the daily relations for almost twelve years. You can say I've studied human behavior.

Therefore, this is a collection of the most relatable data from the trenches of NCO leadership. These teachings are highly applicable to what we do as NCOs daily. I believe in whatever vision and goals each one of you have. There isn't anything you can't do. Nothing is impossible! If there is something you will learn from my book, it's my perception of leadership. I challenge you to take immediate action. Just like you, I am still learning. I hope that after you have read and applied these teachings, we can share knowledge and further our peer reach. I am looking forward to sharing stories. I am looking forward to sharing how to empower those around you to be led. These views expressed are my personal opinions; my personal thoughts and teachings on leadership based on my own life experiences.

Chapter

1

Leadership

"Position and title don't define a leader, their actions do."

-Harrison Burkardt

Do you view yourself as a leader? There are countless names for positions and titles across the Air Force that are sought to define 'leadership.' We often get discouraged when a 'leader' holds that title or role and does not live up to our leadership bias, or what we expect of a leader. We all know what is right and wrong. Leaders, being the most watched individuals, should always find integrity as an asset. The leader is within us; it's a choice we make daily. A commitment to excellence and application. An excellence in all we do (I'm already starting with the corny dad jokes). Holding a title or position doesn't automatically make one a leader. A **choice** guarantees a leader. No rank, tier, or title can confirm such an honor. As an NCO, choose wisely. You have the choice to be a leader daily. Your actions will influence a new culture of leaders around you. Adapt a vision that inspires growth. Challenge innovative concepts. Never stop your hustle.

BACKGROUND

The way I was brought up could be entirely different from your own experience. Throughout my youth, I was questioned on who my real parents were. "Look, there goes the adopted kid," or "The red headed stepchild," and "Jews can't play basketball." It hurt. I internalized a lot of it. I was always 'too tough' to talk about it. As time passed, I became more resilient. It made me stronger as I struggled through adversity. My background played a role in shaping the person I grew to be. As did yours. How can we know what others faced without asking? Get to know the background of those around you. We all come from different places. By places, I mean a different home. We all have our own set of beliefs and principles. The Air Force welcomes people from all over the world. Diversity is a beautiful thing. Welcome it with open arms. How we were raised plays a significant factor in our ethics and principles. Our traditions carry on into our adult life; what we believe, what forms our beliefs, and our foundation. Leaders come in all shapes, sizes, ethnicity, religions, race, gender, age, and cultural backgrounds. The Air Force is an amazing place to learn and discover these backgrounds. Not only is it a beautiful place to learn, but it is also a rare chance to gather diverse teammates to excel. When situations that go against respecting culture arise, stand up for what is right. This should be almost automatic. Being in the Air Force, we are all on the same team. Your silence affects each team member. Everyone should be appreciated for their diverse background and welcomed on the team.

LIFE EXPERIENCES

At sixteen years old, my sister passed away from brain cancer. I lived in a constant mental fog for about eight years, until life smacked me in the face. My wife and children gave me a higher meaning of self. I promised I would live not only for me, but to honor my sister. To cherish each day and grow to my most optimal level.

We all experience different challenges. Leaders go through various obstacles and overcome them. We all pursue a different trail of life lessons. The life experiences leaders face—the total of what they've gone through to get to where they are now—is a constant reminder of their journey. Leaders are grateful for what life has presented; the good and the bad. No two individuals will ever share the same exact life experience. We may find comfort in similarity, but remember to appreciate those new experiences. Learn from other life experiences. Vicariously live through someone else to seek a better understanding of those around you. Leaders share their life experiences to provide relatable knowledge that provides comfort to everyone listening.

FAILURE

There aren't enough extremities on my body to count the number of times I have failed. Grateful is an understatement to those experiences of failure. Through my failures, I seek others in similar situations to speak with, in hopes of preventing them from going down the same path. As you, being human, have also failed. Share those failures with those around you.

Leaders seek failure. Leaders find pleasure in adversity. Leaders know failure is the quickest route to learning. Everyone fails, but leaders stand out because they know they've failed for a reason. Leaders do not dwell on failure. Leaders recognize where they fall short. Then, build to come back stronger and more resilient than before. Leaders know that failure is the ultimate path toward learning. Leaders seek out failure, for they fear complacency. Leaders not only seek personal failure, but they also look for opportunities to challenge those around them to fail, knowing they will support and keep pushing others to reach their highest potential.

PURPOSE

It took me losing someone I loved to find my purpose. Your purpose and how you come to find it will be unique to you. Spend the time to question what your purpose is. Have you found it yet? Leaders do things with a purpose in mind. Leaders make the right choice based on their purpose. Not only do leaders know their purpose, but they also make everyone else recognize their purpose, too. Leaders have planned their next five moves, because they know where the road leads. Leaders give others a sense of meaning. Leaders find true purpose in all. Leaders know situations in life have been presented to them for a reason—to overcome. It is the path given to them to fulfill their destiny. Leaders are just fine with taking the more challenging path, knowing that when they reach their destination, they will be stronger than ever before.

OUTLOOK

If there is one thing I wake up thinking about, it's always 'everyone has good intentions.' They may or may not. It's not my job to determine that. But it is my choice to choose what my outlook is. Leaders have a different outlook regarding people. Leaders are wise in teaching and learning. Leaders find all others to be teachers in their unique field of expertise. Leaders look for those gifts and assemble a team, where everyone is equal. Leaders learn from all walks of life. Not only do leaders go into situations with a positive attitude, they also go into every situation with the belief that they will learn and grow. Leaders are always ready to confront whatever challenges cross their path. What is your outlook on people?

LEADERS ARE NOT BORN

Have you made the choice yet? Yes, you may be an NCO, but are you a leader? What are you doing to become a leader now? As you have the experience of seeing firsthand, oftentimes your work center needs more leaders. WAPs testing is the way to earn the title 'NCO' in the Air Force. Does that test define a leader? Absolutely not. A lot of Airmen enter the military with a solid concept of what leadership truly is. They are already on the path to becoming a great leader. Don't let your rank catch you up. Provide a safer road for those with leadership fundamentals. Help them sharpen the sword. Remember, leadership is a choice, not a birthright. The same is true for yourself. Leadership can be developed over time, with practice and application. It's a commitment to constant personal development, continual education, and constant failure. We make the choice to be a leader. It is never granted as a permission. Once you have formed your leadership principles, they will mature over time, and thus create a broad spectrum of wisdom.

APPLICATION

Trying something new is difficult. I get it! Nothing is ever easy the first time. If you want to be that person you see in your mind, practice. Apply what you have learned. Leaders apply what they've overcome. The life experiences and obstacles overcome serve as a constant reminder to prevent and comfort those who may face similar events. Leaders do not store knowledge. Leaders learn all they are passionate about and pass it on. Leaders form new habits by learning from failures and mistakes. Leaders are always looking for the sharpest edge to improve themselves and all others around them. There isn't anything leaders learn that they do not apply.

WISDOM

Not only do the elderly have great wisdom, so can you. Through learning and experience, leaders have a unique wisdom. Leaders always seem to say what is needed. Leaders never stop learning. Advice from a leader is always comforting. Leaders seem to always say what is right when giving advice. Leaders pull from a vast spectrum of knowledge because they have studied and experienced many obstacles that life presents. A leader truly knows how to lift an individual's spirits when they are down, thereby motivating them back in the game.

VISION

Have you ever thought about what your leadership vision is? Your vision in other aspects of life? Until I really utilized this term, it was foreign language to me. Where do you see yourself in five years? What kind of leader will you be? How will you lead? I challenge you to start envisioning now! Leaders know exactly where they're going. They've found their calling. Leaders bring others along the way, building teams, and helping people grow along their journey. Leaders cast their vision out, in order for everyone to be a part of it. Everyone is welcome along the leader's journey. Leaders inspire others to cast their own vision. A leader's vision is passion-filled and tailored to their specific background. Leaders truly influence others to apply a mindset of vision to others under their direct scope. It is truly difficult not to follow a leader with a vision.

TRANSFORMED BY A VISION

For some reason, all the negative things I experience get me thinking more than the positive. It fires me up. It motivates me to think of what I can change. How I can be the change. I sat on a lot of those thoughts for a long time, thinking it was someone else's job to fix, to create an open, trusting environment. That's horseshit. We all have the voice to speak up as leaders. Speak up! Just do it respectfully. Leaders become leaders at different times in their lives. Once they have seen and tasted their own unique vision, it often produces a momentum toward their personal principles of leadership. Once leaders gain the sight—their distinct purpose—they cannot go back to being a mere supervisor. We, as leaders, have the gift to motivate others to find their vision, to transform, to help those around us find their vision, and to help them transform into their role of leadership. The Air Force needs more leaders!

CHOICE

You made the choice to start studying to promote, why? What choices have you made to become the leader you are today? Leaders are not born with every gift bestowed upon a human. They are all blessed with different gifts. Leaders know they aren't perfect. Leaders know their strengths and weaknesses. Leaders make a conscious choice to amplify their gifts. Leaders make a choice to lead. Leaders are consistent with character and care. Once a leader makes the choice, looking back becomes difficult.

SHEEP LEADING THE LIONS

Sheep – A person filling a leadership role who lacks leadership skills. The desire to acquire more leadership knowledge is rather low. A sheep shies away from an open mind. Such a person may have questionable character. Their attitude is poor. Team building activities are rare, if ever, in the work center. May give feedback twice a year (initial and midterm). Looks out for their own best interest. You get the point. I'm certain that you do not only get the point, but you also understand what a true leader is. Now, if you can recognize a sheep, help them out. Show them the way of leadership. Prevent them from herding together and staying complacent.

Lion – An individual who may or may not hold a 'significant' rank or title. A person who is driven and extremely motivated. This individual finds creative ways to motivate and encourage people, finds likeminded people to grow with, fights for what is right no matter the circumstance, often has brilliant ideas that are left unheard, looks for others just beginning their journey to mentor. NCOs make the choice to either herd with the sheep standing still, or run with the lions, who are always looking for new heights to reach.

"I'm thankful for the sheep, for it makes me a hungrier lion."

When the choice of leadership isn't made, we see the frustration in culture, we see the bias become stronger and stronger, we see the sheep leading the lions. Yes, I know it's frustrating. You'll question it until you turn blue in the face. Outlook is a massive factor, change it. Change your perspective to finding the best in the bad. Being a lion, you're there for a reason—to be that NCO who leads. You've been blessed with this adversity—difficult situations that were placed in your life to ensure growth. Consider this winning the leadership lottery. Grow and learn; take it all in. Respectfully try to improve situations that you can. Take the time to write down what you can improve and what you'd do in these moments of frustration. The leader isn't always the boss. Be strong. Be the leader I know you are. Those around you need it more than you truly know. Not making the leadership choice is in your control. **You cannot control others, but you can control yourself**. The more time you spend focusing on the lack of leadership skills in others, the less time you'll focus on improving your own. Stay on your path. I promise, you'll make it through stronger than you know! Be a lion!

LEADERSHIP AT THE TOP

Just like the telephone game, at the last communication link of the chain, sometimes the original message isn't received. The culture, ethics, heart, and principles start at the top. You can control your scope. Ensure you're aware of the behavior and actions you display. You're now a target. All eyes are watching. All behavior shall follow. You have most certainly heard that saying, 'lead by example.' This is a prime example of how everything rises and falls on leadership at the top. Be the best leader you can be. Keep working on it daily. Keep it in mind as a constant reminder that everything you do trickles down the chain and has an impact.

IMPRESSION

Be you. Don't hang the uniform up as soon as you get home to be a completely different person. Consider every engagement and human interaction as though it were a first impression. First impressions are crucial. Within thirty days of contact, you should know what to expect from a person. For instance, if our new flight chief is a badass in the first thirty days, we can confirm they will more than likely continue to be a badass for the duration of their assignment. Some grow, try new things and change from PCS to PCS. But normally, what you see is what you get. People aren't dumb. After those thirty days, it's difficult to change the impression you've given, so make the most of those thirty days. Some people don't even give thirty days, they may only give one. However, if you do not feel that you are getting their true impression, inquire respectfully. Get to know that new individual. Do not make assumptions quickly. Maybe you can be the change that leader needs.

INFLUENCE

Set the example, and lead by the example you set. The bar that you set should be measurable at all levels. There should be a bar for each criterion you rate on and are rated on. The bar may start at any level. Just as a pole vaulter jumps over that bar, over time, you should set the bar higher and higher, as, subsequently, jumping a particular bar would get easier. You've now put in place what to follow. You've set the bar high. You've set the standard that you will continue to reach higher. To watch and see others follow this process is humbling. Be that NCO! Without a bar being set, what are you truly measuring or doing to ensure growth? How can you fully evaluate performance? How are you influencing change to be brought about if you have not set the standard? Influence innovation. Influence acceleration to change in all spectrums of your workplace.

LEADERSHIP IS AN ART

There are so many different styles of leadership. Once you practice and apply what you've learned, you will form your own leadership style. By reading and trying out different forms, you will find what fits best with your unique traits. There are different definitions and styles you can learn through ALS, but they often don't define what a leader's true potential is. Each of us has a unique personality, character, ethics, morals, motivators, and vision. Leadership cannot be defined by a single word. Leadership cannot be pinpointed to an exact science. It is truly unpredictable. Leadership is a beautiful art. We all paint our own leadership pictures daily. If you haven't started, pick up the brush and start painting.

VULNERABILITY

People's perception of strength is related to dealing with issues and getting through them untouched. To be deemed as 'strong,' one must hide their sorrows. We mask a lot of what we go through in life. We hide suffering and loss, personal trauma and mistakes. In the Air Force, feelings are not normally a topic of discussion. Unless it's a mandatory event, no one feels comfortable with it. But why not? Being relatable, being human, and having the courage to voice what you have been through can save lives. True strength lies in sharing those stories. True bonds are built with courage. An NCO has stories. Challenge yourself to share. Try new approaches to lead by story-sharing. Engage the courage in others by your example.

PERSONAL DEVELOPMENT

This is essential spiritually, mentally, physically, and socially. Leaders work to improve in all aspects. The more these areas are worked, the faster your current shall flow. When heavy boulders of life try to block your path, you will flow under, around, or eventually break through them. Great NCOs strive to improve in all areas, knowing that at any time challenges can arise, and when they do, they will be ready and resilient to overcome. What do you do now to build these pillars of personal resiliency?

PEOPLE WATCHING

Leaders watch what their people are doing to acknowledge their great work and behavior. Leaders seek to find those in the act of doing what is right, not what is wrong. They know people are doing the best they can, always. Leaders watch to see where they can remove obstacles and help others. When an indication of mentoring occurs, the leader does not allow a member to become stagnant. The leader provides guidance. Leaders find other leaders. Leaders bond together and grow. Leaders add others to their team, and leaders work together. Leaders do not wait for help to be asked from them. Leaders recognize where help is needed, and then help accordingly. Leaders do not have to watch what their people are doing to know they're doing the right thing. Leaders trust their people and give them space to innovate. Leaders allow space for individuals to form their own leadership practices.

Reflection Points

- What is your definition of a leader?
- What leadership qualities do you apply daily?
- When did you choose to become a leader?
- What defines a leader?
- What leaders do you aspire to be like?

Key Takeaways

- Rank, title or position does not guarantee a leader.
- Leadership is a choice.
- We paint the masterpiece of our own leadership style daily.
- Always strive to increase your sphere of influence.
- As a sheep, it's difficult to lead a lion.
- Establish your vision.
- Build your own set of leadership principles.
- Stand by your personal core values.
- Speak up for what is right.

APPLICATION

Over the past few years, I've found that the Airmen ask the best questions. The Airmen have been telling us what they want, what they look for in an NCO, and what they expect. There's no limit to the growth you can achieve if you ask the right questions. The Airmen know. We come in with hope and a desire to change, but sometimes, we lose sight of that dream. Let the Airmen have a voice, and value it. No two duty stations or people are alike. Evaluate and understand exactly what your people need. Every person requires something different. As is the saying, leadership is an art. A different situation may require a different form of art. Take the time to survey Airmen, by asking the following questions:

- What is your definition of a great supervisor?
- What qualities make someone a leader?
- What happens when a supervisor cares?

Follow through. Asking the questions to sit on them will do diddly squat. Apply their answers into direct action. If someone asks you to do something and you don't, how do you think it feels? How do you feel? When you've vocalized your wants and needs, and nothing comes into play, follow through with what you've listened to and apply it!

Chapter

Mindset

"Get out of your head and into your life."

- Gary John Bishop

Mastering the mind unlocks endless possibilities. Everything we think, dream, and wish for can come true by expanding our mind's power. Does your mind match with what your heart speaks? Is your mind focused on what others want you to be? Or is your focus on who you aspire to become? You can do anything you put your mind to, rank or not. Fulfill what you love, be the best at focusing on where you want to go. Take every life experience and person you meet with a distinct purpose. Connect the dots. Sometimes, things really do happen for a reason. Learn from all adversity life places on your path. We have so many gifts right in front of our face. Do you recognize yours? The choice is solely in your hands to unlock the power of your mind. Once you've harnessed the gift, you'll be transformed forever. Nothing will stop you.

SUBCONSCIOUS MIND

'*Think it into existence.*' We have heard this saying for years. But how long have you applied it? For some reason, I've done this for years and didn't really think about it until I started reading. When I was sixteen, I'd lie in bed and imagine myself being on stage as a vocalist. While listening to music, I'd envision myself being the vocalist of a band. Those thoughts became clearer and clearer. They became more vivid. I never imagined, at that time, that I'd have a musical career, one record label deal, two tours, and countless memories. Once I realized through reading that I could give back even more, I started envisioning a book... And here we are. At night, think of what you want in life. Turn off the stress and worry. Give yourself your full attention and thought. You really must be at peace and focus on your vision. I'm fascinated to know what you can envision for yourself. The same applies for those around you. Share the power of the subconscious mind. Being a great NCO doesn't just encompass supervisory roles. Being a great NCO is about expanding the minds of others.

GROWTH MINDSET

How disciplined are you when it comes to growth? Do you often notice yourself not receiving feedback from others well? There's much talk of the difference between a growth mindset and a fixed mindset. A fixed mindset can be summed up as 'stuck in their own ways,' with no desire to learn, grow, or change. While a growth mindset entails striving to continually grow and learn. To be a great

NCO, you should not only practice a growth mindset, but plan and preach it. Schedule what you'll learn monthly, quarterly, and annually. Create a theme of the month for growth and make it fun. Make daily checklists. Plan your next five years. Take control of what you shall learn and grow into. Teach what you've learned to others. Create circles and networks of people building their growth mindsets together. Go into every new situation in life with the purpose to learn. You will be amazed at the results.

THINKING BIG

We often get wrapped up on retirement. 'Twenty and done,' and 'I'm starting the countdown.' While I agree this is quite the accomplishment, you should be very proud of serving your country. What's your big plan? Life and dreams can still be lived out during and after the Air Force. I've never heard, "I'm going to retire and sit on the couch all day." But I have heard various retirement plans, and I always ask, "You have these amazing gifts, why not pursue them fully?" If you think small, you shall receive little. If you think big and are realistic, you will work toward it and receive as well. Again, your choice! But you've got twenty years or so to start making moves and thinking big! The sooner you start, the better! Remember, no realistic thought is too big. Most of the time, most realistic thoughts are too small!

TWO VOICES

Maybe it's just me—hopefully not—but there's a voice in my head that speaks about the future; a voice that wants to go further, a voice that tells me anything I want to do is within reach if I work toward it. The other voice, at times, will be a hindrance, a nuisance.

It will tell me I can't and that I'm not good enough. When you start allowing that negative voice to speak, it clouds your judgment. The negative thoughts keep you stuck; stuck on the same negative things. Learn which voice is more critical to your happiness. Silence the voice that brings you down. I don't know your past, but I'm sorry for what has spurred that voice to become louder at times. Focus on the voice that lifts your spirits and draws out the best of your emotions. Control the voice that holds you down.

CONTROL

Just like you choose which is stronger between the two voices, you also choose what you feed. People can say anything they want. We are all allowed our own path. People may not know or care about how they're coming off, but respectfully explaining where you're coming from can change the playing field. Sometimes, people just don't agree with our values, and that's okay. Just remember that what they're saying has nothing to do with you. You know you better than anyone else. That's not your path, so do not allow it to guide you. Control your life and happiness. Do not allow others to usurp that control. Find your unique path as an NCO. Reset. Remember the good in your life. Take a second to breathe and focus on the now. Come back. Now, keep walking your path.

FOCUS

Social media does an excellent job of identifying our algorithm of focus. As soon as you open an app, social media pinpoints what you spend most of your time focusing on. Cell phones track the data on how much life is consumed by cellular interfacing. We often forget the red flags life presents to us daily. We can clearly see where most of our time is focused. We clearly know and acknowledge that it may not be the healthiest choice, but we continue to do so anyway. Check the trends you focus on. Check the time you spend phone scrolling. Is it beneficial to your personal growth? Does it align with your dreams? Are you allowing your mind to think for itself? Or is your phone doing all the thinking for you?

FUNERAL

What would you like others to speak of you at your funeral? What is your eulogy? What do you want to be remembered for? Who would speak at your funeral, and why? Spend some time pondering these questions. What would you want to be said? The actions you take now are a direct reflection of what's to come in your future. It's your choice to make that vision happen with the mindset you choose. That mindset will carry over to the actions you practice daily.

GHOSTS AT YOUR DEATHBED

Imagine all the ideas in your head that you never act on. 'I could never do that,' or 'People will think I'm stupid.' Guess what? You'll never know until you try. Chances are that most people won't even care if you tried or not, but without trying, you'll never truly know yourself, and what your destiny and passion may be. Imagine lying on your deathbed with the ghosts of all the ideas you did not attempt. 'You could have written that book,' or 'Why didn't you apply for that job?' The list goes on. The more ideas you allow to fester in your mind, the more idea ghosts will be present at your deathbed. Take more risks. It'll be scarier looking back at what you should have done, than looking into the future at what could.

INVEST WITHIN

There is no greater return on investment on anything other than yourself. Spending money on monetary items is often extremely rewarding. Guess what? Spending money on your personal inner development is even more rewarding! Gaining more knowledge to become a greater human, becoming a subject matter expert in financial management, life coaching, personal training, therapy, anything that has to do with self-improvement is worth way more than a box of chocolate any day of the week. These practices we pay into are often what we truly love to do and invest most of our time in. The more personally developed we are as NCOs, the more helpful we will be in passing the knowledge on to soon-to-be NCOs.

ROBIN HOOD MINDSET

'*Steal from the rich and give to the poor.*' No, NCOs should not be stealing! So, don't even think about it. The analogy I'm going for is, 'learn from above, give to below.' We can be greater than Robin Hood! Stealing anything is never good. Why not breed a culture of willingness to share? Share knowledge. By this, I mean NCOs should be seeking out mentors. With that knowledge, they should be mentoring others! Mentors come from all walks of life. Peers, troops, supervisors… Really, any subject matter expert. This practice should breed into a new climate in your work area. The more knowledge we gain in all aspects of life, the more we can teach others coming up. Establishing an environment of personal development early in one's Air Force career is critical for success as an NCO. Share and provide the knowledge you have learned over the years.

Reflection Points

- How many ideas have you put to the side because of others?

- What is your biggest dream in life? Are you working toward it?

- Do you allow others to get inside your mind? Why?

- What visions and thoughts do you have often?

- Is the positive or negative voice louder in your mind? What steps can you take to stomp out the negative voice?

Key Takeaways

- Don't let others define you, control within your reach.

- Utilize your subconscious mind.

- No thoughts are too big, most are too small.

- Practice positive self-talk daily.

- Dig deeper into ideas, do not bury them.

- Work toward your funeral vision daily.

APPLICATION

Think about the thoughts in your life that have transpired into action. How long were you thinking about them before they happened? What led those thoughts to become actual life events? At night, focus on where you want to be and see yourself in that place. Continue those thoughts. As they become more vivid, write them down. Write down the step-by-step action plan to get there. Take those small steps daily.

Flip side—don't believe it. Keep doing what you're doing now! I'm sure that in ten years from now, things will magically fall into your lap! Your choice!

Chapter

3

Trust

"Trust starts with us."

- Juergen Burkardt

A lot of stressful events happen on a day-to-day basis. The news has something terrible to report almost every hour. Coping with this on repeat becomes a challenge. As humans, we are not immune to feelings or stressors. Oftentimes, being in the military, stress can feel amplified, as if we are the 1% who should be immune to feelings. Finding out a friend took their own life, PCSs, divorce, illness, failing... The list goes on. Can you imagine all those around you dealing with these burdens scared to come let you know? Scared to vent? Scared to be their true self? Scared to communicate anything that's going on with them? A situation where the only reason you find out things is because it's 'mandatory for their supervisor to know.' This can be prevented if you establish trust. You can prevent and reduce life stressors from becoming a burden by creating trust!

FOUNDATION

What have you done, personally, to build a strong foundation of trust to those around you? As an NCO, it falls on your shoulders to be the bearer of trust. You may be an individual your troop has open communication with. You may be the only individual your troop has an opened a line of communication with. This relationship is sacred, it should be treated as an honor. Strong foundations do not occur overnight. Strong foundations continue to become stronger with time. It is crucial to lay the foundation of trust early on into a personal relation. The sooner trust is established, the sooner you can start leading effectively. Not only will your supervisory influence be more effective, but you will also create a safe environment. When a safe environment is provided in the workplace, those with challenges or brilliant ideas are more prone to speak up and feel like a part of the team. Just imagine how many ideas are left unshared because people do not feel valued. The safe environments I've experienced have not only led to great duty stations, but they've also led to lifelong friendships.

INTENT

Humans are damn good at figuring out why people do what they do. Humans are skilled people-watchers. If you're only out for yourself and don't bring others along, it's a direct reflection of your true intentions. There's no reason to step on toes to make rank or win awards. Do the right thing for the right reasons. People are always watching. After a while, people will know your intentions and create their own perception. Be mindful of the intent you cast.

CHANGE WITH THE SEASON (MOSTLY SUMMER)

We go from base to base and experience a different culture at each. Members can be stellar at one duty location and terrible at the next. Do you ever ask why? Often, it isn't that member who's changed, it's those who directly influence their behavior in the work center. The climate changes often in the Air Force. Leaders come and go. Positions rotate. The disheartening fact being that we hear the bad more than the good. Don't allow the seasons to change too often. The more NCOs who influence stellar behavior, the longer the great climate will stay in season. Be that amazing NCO who practices leadership daily, that NCO who has built a foundation of character.

TRACK RECORD

The Air Force is a small community. Things tend to stick. Be extremely mindful of how you are bearing trust. What you do at one assignment can easily bleed over through your entire career. The same goes for if you've supervised nine troops in the span of an eight-year career, and never established trust with all nine. The truth comes around! Do not let it discourage you. Mistakes are made. We are human. Reach out to those you did not establish trust with, apologize, and make amends. It is never too late to make it better. It is never too late to start running on a different track.

TRANSPARENCY

In my early years, I faulted heavily in this realm. I was too transparent and compromised leaders around my work center. I questioned and disregarded a lot of their leadership principles. If you are asked to be honest, let them know what is really happening;

don't bullshit them. If you're asked about leadership decisions or leadership personnel and you speak down on them, it reflects on your character as well. Teams work together, leaders do not bring others down. Give the most understanding transparent answer you can. Everyone is entitled to their own opinion. You don't have to play a role in said opinions. Allow others to formulate their own perception. NCOs should enable and build the most optimal image possible. NCOs should talk highly of others whether they share the same values or not. That is what makes an NCO a true leader in this regard.

FRIEND

'*Friend.*' We don't really hear this term used much in Air Force culture. It can feel like there are invisible lines separating us from those connections. Be ethical, be professional, and certainly have morals, but don't forget the term 'friend' or what it stands for. My 8-year-old son's definition of a friend is 'a very trusting person I can rely on.' I felt that, buddy. We spend more time with those we work with than our families. Let that sink in for a while. Really, let it sink in. If you are not building trusting relationships at work, what are you building at home? Make some friends. Have fun. You only have twenty years to do it! Those Air Force friendships we build are often the most important because they are the most relatable.

UNDERSTAND

Do your best to not assume or blame. You cannot have a true understanding of a situation unless you fully understand what is taking place. Get to know your people, not just 'know them.' "Yeah,

SrA John works nights." What thoughts keep them up at night? What motivates them? What are they into now? Take it deeper. What does the most significant person in their life value about them, and why? We pass the time with a basic understanding of people and think that it's okay. Those basic understandings can lead to heavy assumptions. NCOs should have a higher understanding to best serve what's needed. Imagine what could happen if every link in the chain felt valued; if they felt like each link had a significant purpose and understood that whatever they were doing, mattered.

TRUST IS EARNED

Don't get too far ahead of yourself. Just because you have a single stripe more, don't think it changes much (congrats on $160 a month more). There is nowhere in the AFI that states, 'NCO, trust shall be granted to all those in your presence.' Just like respect, we need to earn others' trust first. View trust as a distinct privilege, answering your nation's call. Look for ways to build trust. Find the good and recognize it publicly. Notice the bad, and privately save that person from others' wrath. You will directly have the choice, daily, to build trust or destroy it.

Public Recognition Example – SSgt Freddie hears about SrA Mercury killing it at work, going beyond expectations to meet a monthly deadline. SSgt Freddie inquires further to learn SrA Mercury was coined by the base commander. The next day, during morning huddle, SSgt Freddy praises SrA Mercury in front of the flight.

(Public Recognition must be meaningful and real, not phony.)

Private Save Example – SSgt Post watches SrA Malone

continuously nod off at work. Knowing group superintendents check the shop periodically, SSgt Post wakes up SrA Malone and privately asks, "Everything okay? If you need to grab an energy drink, I will cover for you. More importantly, why aren't you getting enough sleep?"

(Saves are the easiest way to establish trust. Just make sure you're being genuine. Get to the issue and help them find an answer to solve it).

If trust has fallen upon you, clearly, something is going right. Do not f*ck it up!

TRUST KEYS

Daily, I observe interactions to find there are simple ways to develop trust quickly. Continuous, conscious effort is a key factor. Trust keys are what I have termed these helpful factors to be. There are ways to unlock the heart quickly, ways to exemplify that you can be a trusted NCO. Practice these trust keys daily, for they will ensure you are inspiring an environment of trust for all those in the work center.

Saves – The number of rules seem to be in the upward millions in the Air Force, with a few hundred being added daily, but we must abide by them! A *save* is going out of your way to help educate someone in a caring way on a rule they may be breaking before someone else has the chance to reprimand or lose their trust. Example: You notice that SSgt Kelly's boots are out of regulations. Instead of letting it go or telling everyone, you pull SSgt Kelly to the side, privately, first explaining that you care about the perception she puts off, and that it could simply be a lack of AFI knowledge.

Then you can suggest that SSgt Kelly should get a new pair of boots that align with AFI regulations.

Cover – Things happen in life. When trust is there, you will know as much detail as possible. You will also have to communicate the extent of the situation to your boss. If you can, *cover* for your troop. Allow time for personal and unexpected matters without question. "Don't stress, I got you covered," makes people feel you are a trustworthy individual. They'd more than likely return the favor. Regardless of whether the favor is returned, you have established a bond of trust by doing the right thing.

Inquire – Care. It takes a short period of time to walk down a hallway and strike up a conversation. This should be mandatory. Care more. Schedule time and ask the right questions. *Inquire* with a desire to learn deeply about that individual's inner workings. What makes them tick? Be involved in personal lives, not just supervisory information. You do not need to be a private investigator; you will come off as that if you do not genuinely care.

Remember – If you have been trusted with valuable information, do your damn best to *remember*. You may have been the only person trusted with such information. I cannot tell you how good it feels when someone sees that you remember something important to them. It gives off a keen sense of value. The perception that you truly care enough to remember that person goes a long way.

Keeping it Real – No one cares that I am a TSgt. No one cares that you are a SSgt (well, maybe our parents do). People do care, but they care more about how you make them feel. They care about what kind of a human being you are. They want to know who you really are; your identity and stamp on the world. Solely based on rank, I am proud of everyone who took the jump in enlisting. At the end of the day, *we are all still human*. We all go through life differently. Our stripes do not grant us immunity or change the fact that we are all still human. Communicate with respect and treat everyone highly. Treat everyone equally. Be yourself. Try not to put the uniform on and change your morals and ethics to be a 'better boss' or 'manager.' A true leader remains intact, uniform or not.

Share Information – If you are the best bullet writer the Air Force has ever had, *pass that knowledge on*. This applies to any criteria you are a subject matter expert on. No task is unimportant. A lot of relevancies are normally hidden in those unique studies that are never brought to light. Spend time teaching what you have learned. Invest in people. I've heard many times of people who have these great ideas, but are waiting for the civilian life to make that money. Things happen, life isn't promised. Sharing information normally leads to greater knowledge, because someone gives you a way to improve on your idea. The more ideas we share, the more ideas we challenge others to create on their own. Brains get spinning when group thinking happens.

Praise – People do amazing things daily. What are you doing to find out? How do you find time to catch the good in action? When you do, how, exactly, do you go about *praising*? Be unique. Have fun. Write a note or publicly acknowledge hard work when it is earned. Oftentimes, we can go on an entire duty assignment without being praised. NCOs have direct oversight and choice of providing genuine compliments. The deeper you know people, the easier this becomes. Custom praises by adding certain things that member really values is a great way to show care. It will also lead to significantly higher levels of trust.

EIGHT CHARACTERISTICS OF TRUST

1. **Character** – Your personality reflects your character. Character defines what ethics, morals, and mental picture you paint. The picture you paint of your character is the visible image all others watch daily. The beautiful part here is that you get to be the artist. If the painting inside is dark and ugly, this will cast a shadow over you, making trust difficult to come by. If the painting inside is so vibrant that it beams with light, you will be a beacon of trust. There is no doubt that a person defines themselves solely based on the character they have formed. Think back to the foundation; the habits you have built over time and have developed into the daily actions you take. People with great character/personality have a high chance of gaining trust quickly. Character can be improved. Put your mind to what you lack and work on it.

2. **Credibility** – "My word is my bond." Keep your promises, make sure there is a conscious effort to show up to events. Go out of your way to support and show love to those in your direct channel. What is an NCO even? Now that the rank is bestowed upon you, how are you living it out? Are you exemplifying personal integrity, loyalty, leadership, dedication, and devotion to duty, including upholding Air Force policies, traditions, and standards? Eyes are fixed on what you do more so than ever before, therefore, be mindful of what you represent.

3. **Courage** – Share stories from the difficult parts of your journey, leading up to becoming an NCO. Share stories in

your life that have challenged the integrity of your being. Sometimes, the challenges you've faced can be relieving for others to hear. It can lead to a connection. The adversity you've faced could even prevent it from happening to someone else. Be vulnerable. Be willing to communicate. Do not expect someone else to open up to you if you cannot do the same. Speak truth. Be you. Fight for what is right. Fight for what is right for your people. Be courageous.

4. **Respect** – Make it known that you respect those around you. Go out of your way to show how you practice respect. Giving someone special attention can be looked at as favoritism, but giving everyone around you special attention is fair treatment. Treat everyone as family. Treat everyone the same. Be kind. Respect is earned. "SrA Berry does not respect me." Well, do you respect SrA Berry? Have you made others feel that you respect them? Look inward before you look outward.

5. **Genuine** – Imagine an environment where rank no longer exists. You were selected to mentor the new employee in the workplace, and assigned the task of showing this individual the ropes. Your job is to ensure their success. This should be the same way we view supervision as NCOs. Your rank holds zero value once you retire. The value of your rank equates to a pay scale. Be honest. Share the facts and tell your personal stories. Be ethical while showing your human side.

6. **Humility** – There is a list of things a mile long of things I'm not the greatest at. There is a list just as long of the times I have failed or fucked up. No shame. There's no

reason to hide or act like you don't have such a list. If you do not know something, make that known. Find the answer. If you aren't the strongest at a certain trait, let it be known. Take ownership and accountability for when you are wrong. Personal flaws are a part of being human. Our jobs as leaders are to find those talented individuals in different areas and build an unstoppable team. We aren't meant to do it alone. People will be smarter than you. Find them and remove the obstacles in their way. Support their potential. Humble yourself!

7. **Faith** – I don't know about you, but sometimes, all I need to hear is that someone believes in me. "That's no problem for someone with your thirst for knowledge," or "I believe in you!" Leaders have faith in their people. They speak their faith unto others. I'm not much of a religious person, but I do believe in spiritual power. Belief and faith go a long way. Letting someone know you believe they can do what they love, and pushing them in that direction will make a lifelong impression.

8. **Integrity** – Yeah, yeah, yeah. Integrity first. What a massive concept. It really is. I think we often forget how important it is. The Air Force provides these basic values as a starting point. The practice of integrity should come with solid effort; the art of doing what is right no matter who is watching. People don't have to watch; our actions display what integrity level we hold. The old saying, "It all comes out in the wash," couldn't be more fitting. Become a master of ethics. We all know right from wrong. Stand for the right. Do not sweep the wrong under the rug.

EIGHT WAYS TO LOSE TRUST

1. **Gossip** – What goes around, comes around. The people you gossip to are more than likely gossiping about you to others. One thing I can confirm is that those who gossip cannot be trusted. I would not want to tell you my personal business if I knew you told half the flight. What I can say is, reverse the bad with the good. Speak highly about others with candor behind their backs. When good words come back, they hit even harder. "Msgt Qwerty said you told him I was a stellar Airman." Hearing that is such an incredible feeling. Give it a try. Avoid the gossip. Avoid those who gossip. Airmen will surely not trust you with pertinent, or any, information if you run the gossip train.

2. **Assumptions** – It's weird to imagine that, as an NCO of twelve years, this is still something I experience and witness daily. You do not have to seek facts if you're involved. Knowing your people, having an innate understanding of their personal lives, interests, passions, and goals will help clear potential risk for assuming. Making the mistake of assuming, only to find out you were wrong, can be a hard slap in the face. It can be challenging to recover from, if the issue you've assumed ends up being significant to someone's health or faith. Before you jump the gun, ask what's going on. Communicate! "I'm worried, is everything okay?" or "What's on your mind?" Assumptions should be avoided at all costs. Once you have created an environment of assumption, you taint the workplace. Not many will feel safe enough to communicate or feel very great coming to work. Ask better questions. Stop assuming.

3. **Favoritism** – Hopefully, this is not anything you've experienced. It's never a good feeling to always be picked last. It's even worse when you are killing it, but you're still being picked last. Treat everyone alike. Surely, you will supervise someone. Requirements and AFIs provide guidance on what to accomplish, however, it doesn't mean there needs to be a lack of support or attention provided to all others around you. The best way to prevent favoritism is by treating everyone equally. Throw any biases out the window as soon as they're presented.

4. **Negativity** – If all talk is negative, bad, unenthusiastic, or demeaning toward the Air Force, over time, people will move past it and leave you behind. Things could be way worse. The benefits fact sheet is enormous. Imagine complaining about all the free benefits we are entitled to daily. Be the positive force. Motivate and rally your troop to a higher level. Low self-esteem is contagious. People will gladly want to give it to you, but how long you choose to live with it is up to you.

5. **Lack of Care** – Personally, this is one of my all-time indications that someone cannot be trusted. Lack of concern is a red flag. There are times when we really need to ask what a person has experienced in life. Take a step back. Maybe even extend a hand. As a supervisor, if you do not show care, trust will not be bestowed upon you. If, for some reason, you cannot find it inside you, it's okay. Take the steps to handle you. Find what is creating the lack of care. You always come first.

6. **Fake** – Consistency in behavior tells the story of what to expect from a person. Certain life situations arise and sometimes get the best of us. Treating certain people one way and others another is difficult to watch. Coming into work daily with a new mask makes it difficult to know the true person inside. Being of a higher status or rank should not trigger you to act differently. We should be truly judged on how we bring those up below us. Keep your composure. Find your vision and follow it.

7. **Misuse of Power** – New roles or positions happen seasonally in the military. It doesn't leave much time for continuity. Authority can be difficult to handle at first. Build a strong character from the beginning. Start now. Find peace of mind. Understanding NCO roles and duties can be crucial to how supervisory tactics are played out. Asking, instead of telling someone what to do, works a lot better. Do not hold rank over the heads of those around you. In the next cycle, they could be your peer, and eventually, they could supervise you. No one likes a bully. Keep the toxic leadership culture out of your ethics.

8. **Blame** – Giving someone a new task and not properly ensuring they're trained potentially falls on the trainer. Not informing an individual of an appointment, only to find out they don't show up, falls on the scheduler. Having a 'bad Airman' is normally a direct reflection of a 'bad NCO.' Remember that. No one likes to be blamed. We all know what we have done. Sure, we should be held accountable for our actions and own up to them. But being blamed or made to feel like you have done something wrong is demoralizing.

When mistakes are made, recognize them, motivate change, and leave the individual empowered to find a solution.

Reflection Points

- What does trust feel like?

- How can you enhance your sphere of trust?

- Who do you trust deeply? Why?

- What factors contribute to losing trust in someone?

- How to you develop trust in a relationship?

Key Takeaways

- Create a safe environment.

- Build trusting relationships.

- Utilize trust keys often.

- Never stop growing in character.

- Be an attitude beacon.

- Establish lifelong friendships.

- Create friendships.

APPLICATION

They say it takes four positive exchanges to make up for one bad one. Take a realistic look at the relationships in your life. In which aspects of your life could trust be significantly improved? Go back over the trust keys and go out of your way to utilize one trust key in the next week. Once this has been accomplished, you will notice a difference in the trust between you and the individual.

Continue to utilize trust keys. How strong a bond of trust can you build with everyone around you?

Chapter

4

Emotional Intelligence

"We treat people how we genuinely feel about them."

Harrison Burkardt

Human behavior is flawed. This has been true throughout the history of our existence. We go through emotions and deal with various stages of life. It's easy to know what someone feels for you by their actions. When you can recognize those signs, why leave it be? Ask that individual why they are expressing that behavior toward you. Of course, do it in the most professional way possible. Their feelings toward you could be a direct reflection of how they truly feel about themselves. Recognizing their behavior and not helping or speaking on behalf of those behaviors will not change much. As NCOs, we are here to grow and help those around us. At first, it may be a challenge to confront someone, but I guarantee that if done professionally, they will have a deep respect for you. As I mentioned earlier, we all have our own unique style of leadership. **FEEL leadership** is what I've coined to be my personal mantra/style. We all have a voice, a stance, and something powerful to offer. Find your heart, connect the mind, lead the way, and take time to find your own leadership style as an NCO.

DON'T FORGET YOUR TROOPS

You may have a PCS, have a change of rater, separate, or retire. By closing all communications after such events, you have signaled a message that you don't care to that person you were entrusted with. Our culture is determined by our actions. Do not play into it. Do not believe that your actions are not significant. The two or three people you treat with care and concern can multiply to twenty or more. In a few years, it could be exponentially more. Just because everyone else is doing something, doesn't mean it's right. People are important. Don't forget your troops. Check in and see how they're doing no matter where the Air Force takes you. The word gets around that we care. Once other individuals know you are one who cares, they will seek you out for help and knowledge. They may even seek you out just to vent to you. If this is already happening, congratulations. NCOs should all seek to emulate such actions.

FEEL LEADERSHIP

Follow Up – "Never leave an Airman behind." We've heard this multiple times over the span of our careers. How exactly do you practice not leaving people behind? My practice of not leaving anyone behind is by following up. When you know of a situation, ask questions to ensure that person is okay. All concerns brought to your attention are brought to you with importance, thus, treat each concern presented to you with care. Make sure to follow up. If you must write reminders or set appointments in your phone, do it. "SrA Tim is sick with the flu," or "SrA Tim, I know you said you were alright, but can I bring you anything?" Two days later, after SrA Tim has turned down the help, you can inquire, "SrA Tim, I know you've said you don't need anything. I'm just checking in on you. Feeling better? Anything I can do?"

Empathy – Not only should you understand the feelings of others you should also be able to walk in their shoes. Try to feel what they could be going through. We all are human. No one is immune to emotions. Show effort in really concerning yourself in their emotional setbacks. Do not brush aside feelings just because you may lack them. If you are busy, reschedule and ensure you care. Look at it from their point of view, then explain why you can't at the time. Be in the moment. Nothing else should matter when people are speaking to you.

Empower – Any chance you get, you should leave someone feeling better than they started off. Make them feel better. Do not waste your chance. Mistakes are made, but still, you can make people feel better, not worse. Never leave a conversation with someone feeling that you aren't concerned for their wellbeing. Encourage everyone. Support everyone. Affirm that they can do anything they wish to do, and that all it takes is a choice. Give them opportunities for growth. Give them space to learn and fail. It only takes one person to unclip a leader's wings.

Lead – NCOs lead the way. Don't wait for things to happen. Make them happen. If something can be done better, make it better. Set the example. Motivate others to a higher level. Be their deciding factor of staying in the Air Force or separating. All it takes is one NCO to make a difference; one NCO to lead! One NCO who leads can be the inspiration for others to follow.

ENGAGE HEART AND MIND

There's no better feeling than when you've connected with the heart and mind logically and emotionally, and made sound decisions. With experience, you will start to listen to your gut and make decisions based on what you feel is right; what you know is best. Allow your mind to relax and stay calm when making important choices. If the two are out of alignment, decisions are often not as clear. If you get caught up in your emotions, breathe and give yourself time to cool down before you make the move. Look at the heart as one wing, and the mind as the other wing. It takes two wings to fly!

TAKE A WALK IN THEIR SHOES

Take the time to truly and fully understand where everyone comes from, and what they've gone through, suffered, and endured. No two minds are alike. Think about a team-building exercise where everyone shares their most challenging life experiences, and how they've managed to make it through. What advice would they offer in that situation? The perfect chance would be an NCO huddle, where all supervisors share their supervisory knowledge and experiences to enhance the culture for all members around. We can talk a big game. We can make people feel like we are going to do amazing things by them. The true test of time is putting words into action. Be careful to watch the things you say. Make sure that what you say becomes action. If you've forgotten, admit those wrongs. Make amends and act swiftly.

LIVE IN THE NOW

We seem to get so wrapped up in what happened yesterday and what's going to happen tomorrow. People cannot sleep at night due to such high stress levels the military includes. Take a deep breath and focus on what's happening right at this moment. There are beautiful things happening all around us. You will miss the chance of seeing those beautiful things if you keep living in the past or future. What could you possibly change that has happened in the past or future? How much time are you losing daily, focusing on those things not in your control now?

HABITS

Everything you do is a habit formed over a lifespan. If where you're at now isn't where you want to be, change it up! The habits you practice today will lead to success years down the road. Add ten minutes of something new to your daily routine. As a few months pass, you'll notice an extreme difference. Bullet writing came late in my career—eleven years, to be exact. I made a conscious effort and plan to write ten to fifteen minutes a day for an entire year. Approaching the year mark, my bullet writing has drastically improved. Get going on applying new, healthy habits! Tomorrow morning, brush your teeth with the opposite hand, it'll engage more brain power. It will also feel ridiculously awkward. Things feeling that way is a great sign. It's a sign that your brain is being stimulated with new processes. Look for more ways to challenge yourself. You can teach an old dog new tricks.

CONTINUING EDUCATION

We speak in terms of educational advancements. They're extremely significant for furthering your knowledge spectrum. They're seen as a ticket to a 'great job.' When we acquire such degrees on the enlisted side, we often do not get a chance to apply those professional skills. That long-standing joke of, "They hold a degree in underwater basket weaving," is highly relatable. Once one does receive a Masters in a certain area, their AFSC doesn't change. They don't get a bonus. It's an interesting factor, so it makes sense that the Air Force does look at degrees with such weight for promotions. One, stop getting mad about the things you can't change. Two, you should be furthering your education anyway. Third, people spend hours of their time invested in school, why would it not be a promotionally weighted factor? Lastly, most of the time, what you would like to master in takes ten thousand hours. School doesn't provide that. This is where the doctorates of many years have done research and mastered their profession. You can spend those hours learning through books and become a master without a degree. Bottom line, stop complaining about free things. Instead, further your education.

Reflection Points

- What habits that you've formed in your life would you like to change?

- What new habits would you like to add?

- When was the last time you took a walk in someone else's shoes?

- How often do you think about the past or future? Does it keep you up at night?

Key Takeaways

- There is no time more precious than right now!

- The healthy habits you form now lead to great results in the future.

- Nothing shows more care than genuine follow-up and concern.

- Practice empathy.

- Empower and lead those around you.

APPLICATION

Practice gratitude. Take thirty minutes to write down how others have helped you. It's not enough to write it down, let them know! Don't be afraid to recognize those in your life who have made a significant impact. It's a powerful practice! If you're having a difficult time compiling a list, I recommend finding a support group; finding those who love you. Try looking at life through a different scope. There is something to be grateful for in everyone. If you ever lack energy throughout your day, I challenge you to practice gratitude. Genuinely reach out to those who have made a difference in your life. Recognize them for what they've done. You may never get the chance to in the future, so, what better time than now?

Chapter

Mentor

"There is no faster way to learn than teaching what you know."

Harrison Burkardt

SNCOs seem to be the most sought-after mentors, typically because that's what we all strive to be. But is that the next step? Choose a mentor based on where you'd like to be in the next year. Who's there now? The best way to analyze this in the Air Force would be the next rank. The knowledge and processes on how they got to where you'd like to go is still fresh in mind. Professional mentoring isn't based solely on career progression. What about roles or things you'd love to learn? Career Assistance Advisor? ALS Instructor? Wing Top 3 Secretary? Personal-wise? Personal mentoring doesn't solely exist in the Air Force. Mentoring from the civilian force can lead to massive leaps in your workplace's production. Having multiple mentors will increase your spectrum of tools as an NCO.

Think outside the box. Career progress doesn't go from A1C to CMSgt. There are many roads to achieving personal fulfillment. Find your passion and find the mentors who fit your definition of such. Mentoring goes both ways, don't forget that. The mentoring experience may teach you more than you expect. It may open your eyes to who you truly are.

SUPERVISOR VS MENTOR

Just reading these words alone, you can differentiate between which one is probably more effective for growth. When 'supervisor' comes to mind, you think oversight of a human, watching someone's day-to-day work actions, and documenting behavior. It's a very managerial term, which makes sense in the realm of corporate structures. Being a mentor, on the other hand, is giving someone the tools to get to where you are now. Mentors get people to the next level. Mentors guide, teach, and have genuine compassion for getting the mentee to their highest level. Sure, an NCO is deemed to fulfill the role of 'supervisor.' You should be the best supervisor **you** can be. Change your outlook and perspective. Consider yourself a mentor. Supervise and manage your program. Mentor and lead your people.

GIVE THE TERM "SUPERVISOR" SOME CREDIT

The term 'supervisor' may not sound amazing regarding concern for people, but the **roles** of a supervisor are quite valuable. Being a supervisor is mandatory when assigned, but being an amazing supervisor is not. Be the amazing supervisor, the amazing NCO, and an authentic leader. Managerial tasks still need to be lived out as an NCO. An NCO still needs to supervise task accomplishment.

How better can you improve these? Can you implement something better? These are elements that make the leader shine through in a managerial position.

- Setting goals for performance.
- Ensuring duties and processes are understood.
- Rule compliance.
- Utilizing corrective discipline measures.
- Receiving complaints/solving problems.
- Writing EPRs.
- Initial/midterm feedback.
- Benefits fact sheet review.

WORDS LIKE DAGGERS

"My troop is so lazy."

This is just a reference quote on how NCOs speak poorly of their people. Noticing your troop is lazy, talking about it, and not doing anything about it makes you equally lazy. You're the NCO leading the way, so you're now the lazy leader. Congratulations! Stop talking down about your troops! It only reflects poorly on those talking. If you notice something, help to find a solution. Words come back around, and they hurt. Talk to the individual directly by 'handling it at the lowest level' in the most professional way. Show that respect. Again, find a solution. Act. As NCOs, if we recognize that someone is lazy, we should probably challenge them to be more productive, make their environment better, and lead them to higher levels of success. It is great that you recognize their behavior. In fact, many do. Only a few will act; only a few will transform others. Be that NCO with great leadership. Make a difference when you can!

"ALS didn't teach me anything."

ALS was an introduction to leadership. The Air Force was nice enough to give you a few weeks out of work to lay the foundation. Nothing is learned in a few weeks. Nothing that isn't practiced and applied over time will be mastered. There are countless books, seminars, professional development programs, mentors, leaders, and classes in which you can invest in to learn. The problem will remain if you don't want to learn. Be mindful of what you say. When I hear folks complaining about not being given tools, it sounds like, "I don't care about becoming a more knowledgeable and better leader. If the Air Force isn't going to teach me, I certainly won't." Read that back. How does it sound to you? Attend a professional development course and bring your people in. Learn and grow together. The most important question you must ask yourself is, 'Do I actually want the knowledge? Or am I just complaining?' You are self-identifying that you do not have the knowledge, so, why not go out and get it? You have talked about others and now, yourself! Step up to the call! Without that knowledge, you cannot build those who wish to become an NCO directly in your chain. Really, at all. Continue to build and expand your leadership spectrum. The Air Force isn't supposed to pay for you to make the choice.

Tips On Being a Better Supervisor

- **Challenge yourself to be different** – There is no cultural norm unless you allow for it. Check the boxes but go beyond them. We can improve the very inner workings in which we are involved. People are the most important asset to the Air Force. Treat them well! There are tasks we must accomplish as supervisors. There are many things we can add to make for a greater experience. Make a list of some of those differences you can implement. Do it right now!

- **Learn** – What you know can be of great benefit and can enable you to give back. The more information you comprehend, the more convenient it will be for you to translate it through channels. Lifelong learning is essential to success. Lifelong learning will lead to an easier comprehension of the art of supervision. How does it feel when someone says, "Go check," or "I don't know, go look at an AFI"? We all have the minds to seek the answer. Stop being lazy.

- **Care** – Emotions are powerful. Valuing the psychological states of a human being is essential. You know when someone cares instantly. When I knew my supervisor cared for me, I felt a lot more at ease. Things were easier to share. It was safe. I was even more eager to do a better job. When care was displayed, it made me take my tasks more seriously. I've been told numerous times, "The one thing you should never lose is your care for people." I do think people care, although they may have a difficult time showing it. Study yourself. Ask if you care enough for the people that you influence. Take those words to heart.

- **Control Within Your Reach** – Focus on your sphere. Master developing people and provide all resources and allow for growth within that sphere. That sphere being your direct line of contact; those who you work with, and everyone you lead. Treat those you lead like family. Remember the saying, 'Never treat others better than your family.' When the time arises, you'll be ready for the next challenge—a wider scope. If you're spending the time doing professional developments at the wing level, be sure to make the time for those directly around you. Make the time for others to go as well. Inquire if they'd like the resources. Schedule the time, and make it happen. An NCO should be creating an environment where their troop learns and potentially surpasses them. As you gain more insight, be sure to share. Teaching the skills you acquire will only sharpen them even more.

- **Allow Others to Be the Hero** – If you notice a situation that is easily resolvable in your perspective, others may not see it. Line people up to be the hero, let them take the credit. Give them a win. Mediate when you can. Be involved. The same goes for awards. You may have implemented a process improvement or seen different things at your last assignment. Show those who do not have/know the way. Set their minds toward the path of creativity. Accelerate growth in others by believing and providing the tools.

- **Have a Deeper Understanding** – Get to know personal lives and personal triumphs. Remember birthdays and remember conversations. Ask about their families and ask about what is most important to them. Things change often. Keep up on your understanding. Formulate better questions that give you optimal answers to knowing those around you. People love to feel understood and important. If you care, make the time and effort to show it.

- **Celebrate** – Promotion ceremonies are great. It's a good way to show love by making sure you're there. What if you add to the celebration? What if you celebrate personal accomplishments? Birthdays? Milestones? Provide a first day of work custom gift basket. Not only for the individual, but their entire family? Celebrate morning huddles. Come up with a new person to brief every morning. They must walk in while playing their favorite WWE intro song. There's no reason why we can't. It's a great way to show that you really care. Celebrate life. Find new ways—that do not include your typical Air Force tradition—to celebrate. Create lifelong impacts and memories.

"Slow down or you will burn out."

While burnout can happen, be aware of the goals those around you are embarking on. Everyone works at a different pace. Remove obstacles in the way to prevent burnout. Just keep in mind that some personalities don't burn out. Some individuals find their passion and chase it. That passion may be of a higher purpose than just rank. These sayings can come off as disbelief as well. Remember, leadership is language. Be more encouraging!

"You're killing it, how's your family feeling about it? What's on your mind with all your recent success? What's next?"

"What's your goal? What's the game plan with all these tasks you're accomplishing?"

Asking better questions can help bridge a better understanding and get to root causes. Then and there, you can motivate, encourage and be proud. Telling one they may be overworking can set a low expectation. Offer more, coach and give advice on what's next to lead to ultimate success. Implementing questions into feedback sessions are critical for this purpose.

HOW DOES ONE MOTIVATE?

The more you learn what the needs of others are, the easier it will become to motivate them. People are driven by different things. Times change and things happen. Ask what exactly motivates them. If they do not know, help them find out. Establish a bond. Communicate your purpose for finding what their motivators really are.

> **Achievement** – Hardware/trophies, certifications, diplomas. You have to attain a certain level to achieve an award. Air Force-wise, there are many criteria to fit the achievement motivator. There are civilian sector awards that Air Force members can acquire too (colleges, businesses, volunteerism in the community). Become knowledgeable of all the awards the Air Force has to offer and when they're due to flight leadership. You can also go out of your way to create an award for something you notice. Put an award program in place for monthly performance or character. Fun awards can build a team. It can be anything meaningful you can think of to recognize applicable actions. Try to avoid participation trophies. A 'You didn't call in sick today' award misses the mark. Be that NCO who awards character and performance.

Recognition – Acknowledge others for the hard work that's been done. In doing this, you can let others know in a public setting. It can be private too, just ask which they prefer. What level of recognition does the individual fancy? Wing command level or just within the flight? Keep the work recognized in mind. When you recognize someone, you take notice of what is happening. It's simple. Find the good to recognize and do it often!

Job interest – The Air Force has numerous jobs across various career fields. There are titles that one can hold within a flight that change over time, such as cross training, private organizations, preventing burn out from doing the same task for years. Enable the opportunities to allow that chance. Shadowing programs exist. Coordinate with your flight leadership to allow the breadth of experience to see what different jobs are out there.

Responsibility – Some people really love to have more responsibility. They're more mature or possibly experienced with the subject matter. Or they just love responsibility. Be creative. If programs around the group are available, throw their name into the hat. If you can allow for your troop to cover you and learn what you do, allow them to do so. Set them in the places they best fit.

Advancement – Promotions play a heavy factor in Air Force culture. Set people up for success. Make sure they're getting to the next level prepared. Teach them how to write bullets, explain supervisory roles, share more information than expected. Ask them if they feel prepared. Then dial in on where they need to work to get to the next level to the best of their ability. Promotions drive a lot of people's motivation. Try to help them find their right reason to seek advancement.

MENTOR

NCOs are mentors, whether they know it or not. Every task and role you've performed up to this point can be a crucial insight for someone else. Personal life experiences often lead to different forms of mentoring, for instance, dealing with loss, divorce, suicidal thoughts, PT failure, etc. These can require different aspects of mentoring. Know what you are an expert at, and give back. Prevent others from making the same mistakes you have. Provide guidance, so that they do their tasks more thoroughly, ensuring that they do not stumble often. Personally, I'm an expert at not making SSgt. It took me five attempts. Now, I go out of my way to educate and mentor those prior to WAPs testing, to equip them with what I didn't seek in order to make sure their mindset isn't like mine. You've been blessed with experiences and life, too. Pay it forward. Mentor more.

WHAT A MENTOR DOES

Lights the path – 'Been there, done that.' As I mentioned previously, a mentor is someone who has been down the path you are wanting to travel. This individual makes sure that your route is lit, and that all you need to do is follow suit. Follow where the light leads, and the end of the tunnel will become brighter and brighter as you reach for accomplishment.

Holds people accountable – As with feedback, a mentor finds what is to be achieved in the relationship and discovers where the journey is going. If the mentee is not following through and acting upon what they desire, the mentor should vocalize what standards are not being met in accordance with the goals set, as a constant reminder of what the task at hand is.

Challenges – Seek intentional failure. You'll get to know who you mentor well. Ask where they struggle and where they need growth. Set them up to directly overcome and conquer those challenges. They may fail, but learning will come fast, and confidence will follow. The things we fear in life are indications of what we need to face the quickest. Accountability partnership—it's a two-way street. If the goal is to get better at a task, join in. Go to the gym together or text when you've arrived. Apply this to other tasks. Keep a habit tracker—the example I've seen most is tracking your spending weekly. At the end of the week, you may notice that your Starbucks visits are $234. Track habits that can lead to better personal character traits. Track negative mind talk to increase self-love. "This week, I told myself I smelled awful fifty times." Having data to improve on helps. The following week, you can say, "This week, I told myself I smelled terribly thirty-five times." We can do better by improving on what we acknowledge.

Experienced – Find the subject matter experts in where you see yourself in a year. It could be yoga, speaking a different language, becoming excellent at excel spreadsheets... Anything, basically. Whatever it may be, find others who explore different practices and tactics. The more knowledge and forms of the art, the faster you will master what you're looking to learn.

Coaches/teaches – Motivate with speeches and positive affirmations. Give clear positive step by step direction of what's to be accomplished. Have passion when you are teaching tasks. Know exactly what information you are teaching. Know exactly what to convey to each unique individual so that everyone can grasp the subject material.

Encourages – Support is a huge factor. Show up to outside events, not just those the military provides. When failures occur, be there to listen and guide to keep moving forward. Have faith and believe through the entire process until the goal is reached. Encouraging thoughts and people are those you should surround yourself with.

Motivates growth – As one grows, one may not notice how far they've come. A mentor watches the process and tracks how much you've grown and how far you've come. They can see potential. They can also determine what level is to be reached next. A mentor should push you until you've reached maximum growth in the desired area of focus.

Stretch – Mentors stretch you in different directions. Just because you see it one way, doesn't mean there aren't multiple ways to do things. The more you stretch, the more things in life you will touch, thereby furthering the reach in which you influence and giving you a perspective beyond what you could ever imagine.

Network – Mentors can offer who and what they went through to get where you need to go. Having already gotten there, they may have a network or resources available to you that can open doors. Now, all you must do is walk on through. This also allows and creates more opportunities to help those around you when a similar situation presents itself. You will have the opportunity to provide the same resources.

LEARN WHAT YOU DESIRE

You will inquire about and learn what you truly seek to gain knowledge in. You'll gravitate toward the things you are most interested in. Most people seek knowledge in the realm they love. Often, it may seem like it has nothing to do with military relations. Is there any way you can apply it? Professional development isn't for everyone, but make the conscious effort to attend what interests you. There's always at least one thing you can take back to your flight. Apply the knowledge and help someone who wants the information. Find out what those you lead desire to learn. Push them in that direction or bring it to your workplace for certain days that allow for it.

COLLABORATION

You have heard the term 'networking' throughout your entire career. Networking is an essential tool because you gain the information to reach those who may be able to help with the task at hand. 'Collaboration' is a term not heard often. Collaboration is when you utilize those network channels into action, when you form teams with individuals who have a distinct knowledge that can work on a joint project. When you do go out and network, I challenge you to connect those pieces like a puzzle. Work on bigger projects to enhance the base you work at. Create things in the community. Give back to the Airmen.

BOOKS

People aren't always readily available. It's not fair to expect someone to drop everything to hear you out one hundred percent of the time. A quick and easy way to gain insight and advice is by reading. Those who've made it to where you desire share their knowledge through books. There are countless books on every subject or area of interest you can imagine. Research the best books on that topic. Get grinding on reading, expanding your brain function, and reducing stress. If you aren't a reader, don't worry. Ease in. Start with just a few pages a day, then build your endurance. The sooner you start, the less time you will spend looking back, regretting that previous choice.

A PATH TO SUCCESS

Success is defined by your own personal beliefs and goals. Once you find your sole identity, things really do come together. Do what you love. Do not compete with others. Find where you want to go. Find competition within yourself to get there. Work hard. Don't let the voices of others change your course. Everyone goes and grows at different rates. Support and encourage their path. Focus on happiness and self-fulfillment. This will directly translate how you go about motivating others. Remember, it's not all about the stripe. Goals and visions go past the Air Force. What are you doing to set your troop up for success after their military career?

Reflection Points

- In your life, who do you consider a mentor? Why?

- Have you ever gone out of your way to mentor someone?

- What local resources offer a mentorship program?

- What qualities do you look for in a mentor?

- How can you become a better mentor?

Key Takeaways

- Be the greatest supervisor you can be.

- Apply mentoring tactics to NCO roles.

- We all learn what we desire.

- Every path is different, find your own.

- Find motivators in people, then motivate them!

- Gain insight from books.

- Take being a supervisor to a higher level, defy the standard.

APPLICATION

First – Find a mentor, seek someone who will benefit the needs you seek most. This does not have to be military related. It can be anything you truly desire to fulfill personally. It's difficult to ask a role model to mentor you due to the fear of rejection. Remember, there are plenty of fish in the sea. The right mentor will be thrilled to say yes. Being asked to be a mentor is a privilege and an honor.

Second – Remember, you were the one who sought out the knowledge. You asked for the mentorship. Make sure you are actively committed to the process. Schedule the time and make it happen. Come with exactly what you would like to gain from the mentoring experience. Bring questions to ask. Explain where you would like to go exactly.

Third – Apply the knowledge of the mentoring in what you do daily. Share the knowledge to those around you. Seek more likeminded folks who want the same knowledge. Now, you have become a mentor.

Chapter

6

Communication

"The most important thing in communication is to hear what isn't being said."

Peter Drucker

Throughout an eight-hour workday, fifteen minutes of communication is remembered. Everyone has a desire to remember a different fifteen minutes of their choosing, which could have zero relation to work or anything you've said. People remember how you make them **feel**. The communication you convey changes moods, sets the tone, opens doors, or can shut things down quickly. Any, and all, exchanges will not be remembered precisely by what was said, but how you have made others feel. Communication could take a lifetime to master completely. We make the mistake of listening to what others communicate to us about those we are directly in a relationship with. We do not ask the right questions, nor do we listen for the right cues. If we just focused on our reach of communication directly to those involved, we would solve a lot of miscommunication and perception issues. We often judge others by their history; what has been communicated about their past. We don't ever bother to discover what they are truly into now.

ATTITUDE

We expect our troops to show up daily with a perfect attitude. Do we ever look at our own? Actions are a telltale sign of what you shall receive from an individual. People will treat you how they feel about you. People will act upon how they genuinely feel. Attitude is a continuous effort and practice if the desire is for it to be positive. Human emotions cannot be removed, as hard as you try to push them aside. Our attitude toward others and how we treat people is a huge factor in communication. The way you express yourself daily is a direct reflection of what you communicate to the world. Positive translates to a good attitude, negative the opposite. You silently communicate the kind of person you truly are with the attitude you convey. Do you find yourself striking up conversations with people who are positive or negative? If you struggle with attitude, there are ways to improve it. Attitude is a critical factor in life. It isn't something taught or focused on. Don't get me wrong, it's not easy to always have an immaculate attitude. But you can get damn close with practice and effort. Here are a few ways to improve your attitude daily:

- Investing twenty minutes reading positive books/quotes/poems daily.

- Listening to motivational speeches.

- Avoid energy vampires (negative folks). When negativity is a routine, it can wear on your energy. Be mindful of how much time you spend with such energy. Find those who give you positive energy and drive you to become better.

- Don't take yourself too seriously. Laugh a little! Most of the time, you can drop what you are working on and come back to it tomorrow. With people, it doesn't work that way. Enjoy the moments and make memories.

- Get a different viewpoint/perspective. Reverse mentoring is where you challenge your personal views. Expand your mind to the opposing side. The more input from various points of contact you receive, the better perspective you shall receive. Sometimes, all it takes is asking a question.

- Avoid victim mentality at all costs. Shit happens to us, consider it a blessing in disguise. Use those obstacles of adversity to become better and grow. Problems can result in opportunities if looked at that way. Instead of looking at the world like it's against you, try looking at the world as though it is meant for you.

- Dominant thoughts rule the day. We have two voices in our head, one that envisions and knows where you could go, and the other voice that tries to keep you down. When that voice tries to shut you down, shut **it** down.

- Face your fears and grow. What triggers anxiety and fear for you? Those are the challenges you must seek and overcome. Public speaking, leading a professional development program, even working in a new work center are possible triggers. Life is difficult. Life isn't fair. Tackle the difficult things first so you can focus more time on the most rewarding things.

- Change your thinking. You have the power to control how you speak to yourself. Practice self-love, especially mentally. Stop bringing yourself down. You should know you the best. You should know yourself enough to stop wasting energy on the thoughts that make you stagnant. This may take time. Get to know yourself better to have a deeper understanding of what self-talk may be negative.

- "How are you?" This is the funniest observations to watch on Mondays. Responses are normally "It's a Monday," or "God, it's been a rough week," then, "WHAT?! We are only one day in!" Instead, switch it up. "How are you?" then, "I am fantastic!" Your mind affects what happens physically— what you think will have a high chance of coming into fruition. The universe hears and answers, based on how you speak to it. If you tell yourself this is the best assignment you'll ever have, you will make it that. If you tell people your Mondays suck, they probably will. Same goes for how you paint pictures of others. Be mindful of what you say. Be generous with care.

- Stop complaining. Or try to! Look at the good in life. You've come this far. There are way more things in life to be grateful for. The time spent complaining could be time spent appreciating others. As an NCO, minimize complaints, especially in the work center. If the issue is so bothersome, find a solution.

LEADERSHIP IS LANGUAGE

Everything you say or do not say reflects what you stand for. If the conversations you have are passion-filled and meaningful, you will be held in such regard. When you do not speak up at the right time, your leadership ethics can be brought into question. Voice what is right and stand behind what you believe. Over the years, a common line I've heard is, "We are a family." This can sound incredible. We must keep in mind that everyone's definition of a family is different. If we are a family, how do you define that exactly? Another interesting example is when someone is new to the flight and talks about their personality. Shortly after, you're looking for those traits and don't see them. The language we translate transfixes thoughts of hope. Word choice, or lack of words, can oppose hope. Be selective of what you convey, and how you do it. If we do not follow through or if our words fall short, we will be judged even more critically. The actions by which we treat people may be the most significant form of communication, for we are communicating to that individual how we truly feel about them. Be aware of what you say, how you say it, and what you're doing in relation to your language. Encourage ideas and welcome the minds of others to play a role on the team.

LISTENING/VALIDATION

When someone comes to you, they typically respect what you stand for. The measure of the NCO you are amounts to how you treat those you lead. When anyone comes to you directly, they want you to validate their ideas and feelings. You have been blessed with this privilege. Sometimes, it's best to simply listen. Or you may need to inquire deeper about the situation. Help who has come to you to formulate their own answer. Validate what feelings they may have, good or bad. Be relatable and be honest. The most helpful tool I've learned is asking, "What's on your mind?" It opens the conversation up for individuals to finally get frustrations off their chest. The question needs to be asked with genuine care—a desire to truly understand. When the topics have been relieved, you can go further with a simple, "Go on," or "Please continue further." Validation is a massive piece in communication that we lack. Here is why an NCO should apply such methods.

- **Become an advice magnet** – By allowing others to vent and help formulate their own answer to the situation, they will believe you have bestowed upon them a secret to fixing their problems. They had the solution before knocking on your door. What was more valuable was the time invested listening and validating their concerns. How often do we convey, 'I'm busy,' or have phones glued to our face when a critical issue could be brought to the surface? Put the phone down! Become unbusy. Listen!

- **Liked among many** – When someone is heard and understood, they feel a deep bond of connection. No one is perfect. Being able to relate when a situation is difficult is sometimes all they are seeking.

- **Master empathy** – Become one with their situation. Saying, "Damn that sucks, hope you figure it out," leaves people wondering if you really care. It leaves them feeling like the listener does not want to listen any longer. Saying, "Damn, that sucks, I can understand you're upset. I get that way when my supervisor yells at me, too," shows concern. Practice empathy. You may have that extra stripe, but we are still humans.

- **Engage fully** – During the conversation, have patience. Allow them time to speak, do not jump into answering. Maintain eye contact. Remove all distractions. The more you are engaged, the better you will come off.

- **Honesty** – If you can't relate, let the individual know. You could say, "I've never experienced this. I can imagine how difficult it must be. Please explain more so I can have a better understanding." Just keep it real. Be honest. Making up stories will make the situation worse for the individual speaking. Your credibility level will decrease significantly.

- **Time** – If you do not have the time when you've been sought out for advice, schedule the time. You could say, "Right now, I have to finish this for a deadline. Your concern is highly important to me. Can you come back in twenty minutes?" We can't be available 24/7, but we can communicate that we will make time to be available for the concerns of others.

- **Show Appreciation** – That individual could have picked someone else to vent to. Stop looking at it in a bad way. **You** were chosen to listen. Thank those who have allowed you to be a part of their lives.

FEEDBACK

Feedback should not be solely used to check a box. Accomplishing an initial and midterm is doing just that. When your troop fills out their feedback form half-assed, they more than likely have little confidence in your knowledge or ways to help them succeed. They may say, "Why fill this out if they aren't going to help anyway?"

Feedback can be uncomfortable at first. If your feedback is expressed with true care and concern, it should be received well. It comes off easier if you lead, explaining your concern and care, and why you are bringing this to their attention. Looking out for the others' best interest should always be the end goal. Feedback is critical to growth. Being at the middle tier of the rank structure, you have the benefit of getting feedback from all directions. Your peers are a great resource to ask for feedback. How could you be a better team player? Improve your section? Mentors and supervisors ahead of you can give great feedback, too. The best feedback usually comes from those we take care of. They can evaluate what we aren't doing, and how we can treat them best. Most of learning how to be a better leader and NCO comes from a deeper understanding of what your people need. Feedback should be determined case by case. When feedback is needed, it should not be ignored or put off until mandatory. Feedback should be consistent and supportive. ALS provides the basic understanding of how to conduct military feedback. There are several ways to improve growth, and an important one is adding more dedication to your feedback practices.

A FORM OF CARE

If you are willing to, take the time to recognize where someone can improve. That shows you have invested in their improvement. There is often a fear of giving someone feedback, the fear of someone not receiving what was heard, well. You fear they'll think you're an asshole for recognizing where they could improve. I think it's scarier to let feedback go unheard. Supervising an individual for six months to six years and not relaying anything keeps an individual at a standstill. In life, we should be growing, not stuck in one place. Here are steps and questions to make your feedback more effective.

Prepare – Preparing doesn't just come with filling out forms, getting documents ready, or finding extra things to add. Preparing for feedback is investing the time to see and understand who your troop really is. Find where they are passionate and the kind of person they are in general. Spend the time to get to know someone. It will lead to a much better response to required feedback sessions. They will go the extra mile to fill out all blocks of the feedback form to their best ability because they trust that you'll provide the tools to follow through.

Last three EPRs – Try to look over what has been done and built, and make sure there's new things for the upcoming reporting period. Find where they are driven and find what area needs more growth. Seeing their last three EPRs can help roadmap their next ones. Show them where you expect them to be. Do not let them go in blind. Explain what you expect of them, and how they will get there, step by step.

Fitness – Ask those questions! Learn what your troop enjoys doing in their free time. If they have vocalized they enjoy gaming and slamming Mountain Dews, it may be an indication they are lacking in the fitness realm. Do not assume! Simply ask. This will enable you to see where the member may require help. Ensure they will meet the standards, or address concerns before testing. Some NCOs do this weird thing where they wait until their Airmen fail at something to start acting. No one says you must run a track or do mock tests. Recognize where they stand prior to testing. Go out and do fun things that aren't mock tests like swimming, biking, hiking, or other sports. There are so many options out there. Finding a new hobby may cause them to find passion in physical activity, which will, in turn, prevent physical training failure. Imagine we all waited until all our teeth fell out to start brushing. There's no good in that.

Be different. Be an outstanding NCO. Ask more than what's required. Here are a few examples of questions to add to feedback. I'm sure you can formulate some amazing questions to really dive deeper into the dreams of others.

- What incentives would you like to see?
- What would you like to see in me as an NCO?
- What motivates you?
- What's your story?
- What do you want to see from my supervision?
- What does the closest person to you value about you?
- What are your dreams?
- What are your education goals or personal development plan?
- What would you like to improve on? Personal and career-wise?

- What are you into now?

- Where do you see yourself in five years?

FEEDBACK TOOLKIT

- **Highlight good work when noticed** – Don't wait to recognize good work! It won't be nearly as effective the more time passes. You may forget the exact details, too! Use these moments as a teaching point. "I noticed you did this in excellent fashion, keep doing exactly that!"

- **On the spot** – There is no reason to wait until a midterm or initial. Let it be known how they are performing. Do not leave the rating scores to be guessed come EPR season. Coach them throughout the grading period. Once you notice where they are lacking or excelling, dial in.

- **Be specific** – "Volunteer more," or "Get better at your job," or "Be a better NCO." Without precise guidance, they will make hopeless attempts at trying to answer what you have mentioned. They could perceive what you said in a completely different way. "I would suggest you volunteer more at the wing level with your peers, maybe hit the 5/6 for a POC event," or "Remember, being an NCO means mentoring your troops. Teach those Airmen what you know. I would like you to mentor your troops on feedback techniques this week."

- **Provide a performance improvement plan** – Outline their strengths and weaknesses. You should know very well what they are lacking and what they are excelling at. Draw out a road map for where they need to go to meet your expectations and be graded accordingly. We should be growing people to improve yearly at the very least. Prevent the questions by providing the answers. People fear asking for help. Custom roadmaps will build a bond and change their outlook if you follow through.

- **Ask how they like to receive feedback** – A lot of people just don't want to hear it, whether it be our duty or not. NCOs, I'm sure, struggle with hearing the cold, hard truth and reality about themselves as well. Cater to the individual based on how they like to receive feedback to ensure it is relayed in the most effective way.

- **Practice empathy** – We forget that sometimes, people just do not know. Sure, we can be fooled, but we will come to find out the truth eventually. We excuse children by saying, "Little Jimmy didn't know any better," but when adults don't know, they're immediately shunned and made to feel stupid. I challenge you to practice looking at adults the same way. For instance, you can say, "Maybe A1C Ryan didn't know."

- **Two-way** – By providing the feedback. If you are doing all the talking, how the hell are you going to know what the individual needs? Ask questions. Gain knowledge by listening to others speak.

- **Focus on performance, not personality** – Do not mention areas in which a person lacks character. Instead, tell them how their performance is contributing to the mission, i.e., what they do versus what they are like.

- **Private** – This should be a no-brainer. Do not give

feedback in a public setting. Praise and feedback are two different things. Sometimes, praise should be done in private, too. But speaking of feedback for the receiver and the giver, it can be uncomfortable. Make it as comfortable as humanly possible for both parties to ensure that what is communicated is well received.

FOLLOW UP/THROUGH

This may be the most important factor. Feedback sessions hold zero weight if you don't close the loop. If someone has trusted you with their dreams, goals, struggles, and life challenges, you'd better make sure you're keeping them accountable to those goals. Remove roadblocks when you can and set them up for success. Network and find what could benefit them in reaching their vision. You may already have the tools to do so. The more we help others with different situations, the more we grow our own toolset. Imagine telling someone your dreams, and they listen and do nothing. It doesn't feel very good. Don't be that NCO.

CRUCIAL CONVERSATIONS

Crucial topics are not easy to address. The more time they go unaddressed, the more drama and tension they build. When you do not confront those involved, more than likely, others will start to figure out the situation, create rumors, and paint different pictures. These are all preventable. That silly saying, 'handle it at the lowest level' is smart, if used accordingly. When issues cannot be resolved at the lowest level, mediation may be required. When you face these challenges as an NCO, decide what's best—the most professional option for the situation. Sit on the topic for fifteen minutes and try not to focus on it too much. Collect your emotions and be logical when you do have to confront someone about an individual. Try not to assume or read between the lines. Look at their perspective first. You may not be completely wrong or right. Bring a solution to the table with benefits for both sides. Never leave a crucial conversation without agreeing to the best common ground.

CONNECT

Laugh, smile, have fun. Be your true self. There are so many of us hiding because of the cultural stigmas. We are normally the factors and reason for why they exist. By connecting, we can further eliminate these from existence. Have a good time, but keep it professional and ethical. Prank one another, dance to music, team build, and help where needed in personal lives. Connections truly last. The stronger the connection, the harder it is to break. At the peak of connection, nothing is impossible. When a team is connected, all members feel safe and contribute their best abilities to the mission.

EXPECTATIONS

Expectations must be there! If they are not, what are you expecting to grade on come EPR time? Low expectations lead to small results. High expectations lead to growth. Be realistic, set the bar high, and make it fun and attainable. Communicate what you're expecting, how they can get there, when it should happen and why they're doing it. It's difficult to justify marking someone down when you have no expectations.

GUIDANCE/DIRECTION

People who are diagnosed with blindness utilize a walking stick to navigate their way around. Imagine being blind without a walking stick. Upon arrival at your first duty station, everything is foreign; processes, programs, rules, regulations, chain of command... The list could more than likely be half this book. How are you guiding that new Airman through the steps? What guidance and direction are you providing for her to not only be successful with your supervisory position but throughout her career? You've provided the expectations, and feedback has been very well received. What is the point? Where exactly is she going? What is the end goal? Why is her EPR important? Why do awards matter? Her next five moves matter, but how you guide her there is the key. Explain your reasoning and the purpose for where you are taking her and where she is taking herself. The same applies for the mission, what the flight has planned and where it is going. Every member should have the knowledge to ensure a clear understanding across the board.

Ways to Prevent Miscommunication

- **Listen intently** – The more actively I am engaged in what is being said, the better understanding I will have. It's extremely difficult to turn your mind off. Try your best to do so! Find ways to clear what is on your mind and focus your attention on the speaker. Repeat key points that have been mentioned, and corelate them to things you are familiar with so you can truly relate and remember. Focus on the now. Give 100% focus on the words being spoken. Be in the moment. Practice mindfulness.

- **Write it down** – The easiest method of miscommunication prevention for me is writing things down, from morning huddles to the daily grind. You may pass by someone who tells you something. Five minutes later, you may forget who told you what. Writing things down is a great way of ensuring effective communication.

- **Circle back** – When someone says something in passing, it may be important. Suggest to the individual that they also email you as a reminder. If you do not remember what was said, follow up with the individual to ensure the message was received accurately. Inform the individual that, sometimes, you forget things in passing. Let them know that what they have said is important and that you are preventing yourself from forgetting.

- **Explain thoroughly** – Details matter. They make those who are being spoken to feel important. The more people are in the know, the better messages can be translated and relayed to others, and the more important they feel. Sometimes, I go overboard and give people the history of certain tasks and where they came from so that they can fully comprehend them. Ask if you're going too far. Communicate that you are explaining so they can better understand.

- **Ask if you were understood** – Ask, "That was a lot of information, my apologies if I lost you anywhere. Did you grasp the information fully?" Be kind. Communicate that if the message was not relayed well, you will spend the time and effort to clarify it. Ask the question, do not assume.

- **Know your people** – Knowledge of people's habits around you and what methods of communication best work for them will lead to optimal levels of communication. Some may need more work with communication than others. Keep in mind that communication is no easy task to master. Spend the time to practice daily.

- **Face value** – Don't rely solely on email. Once you've sent an email, give it some time to get feedback. If it has gone past your time threshold, inquire with that individual in person. They may have been extremely busy working on something or got caught up doing something else. By going to see them, you may be surprised to find that they really are busy. It's easy to forget when we wear twenty different hats. This is also a great chance to get out and see what is going on. Establish a stronger bond. Understand what your troop does day to day. It's difficult to write an EPR when all communication has been through email.

- **Avoid interrupting** – Interrupting can come off as though you are in a rush and have somewhere else more important to be. If you interrupt to make your point, it shows you may not value or believe the one talking is intelligent. It could also cause the one who needs your support to not relay their full message. When asked for an opinion, give it. Allow others to fully express their message before you speak. Pause and ensure they are finished. You will have a chance to speak. Make sure it's the right moment.

- **Allow others to be correct** – We get it. There are points to prove everywhere. If the answer given by someone else is inaccurate, offer to find the answer together. What good do you think it will do to correct someone on irrelevant subjects? When the subject is relevant and crucial to duty performance, find the most effective way to not come off as demeaning when you're relaying accurate information. Making someone feel stupid will certainly not go over well. Think about the last individual who made you feel less than smart. Have you spoken to them since?

- **Repetition** – There are times when what you say goes unheard or is forgotten. It's difficult to remember everything that's communicated throughout the day. If what you've said is important, say it multiple times. In addition, send out an email for continuity as well. Joke around in repetition. Try fun ways to repeat yourself to get the point across. My dad does this with corny jokes all the time. It's easy to memorize those jokes when we repeat them often.

Reflection Points

- How can you improve your communication skills?
- How often are communication loops left open?
- When is the last time you gave someone feedback?
- How often do you provide guidance?
- In what ways do you prevent miscommunication?
- How can you provide better feedback?
- Can you ask better questions?

Key Takeaways

- Provide feedback often—do not solely rely on what is mandatory to provide.

- Prevent miscommunication.

- Validate emotions.

- Don't be afraid to have crucial conversations—the more time you waste, the more frustration accumulates. So, get that shit off your chest quickly!

- Pay undivided attention when you're listening, and listen with the intent to understand.

- Without expectations, there will be no progress.

- Be an ambassador of positivity.

- Work to improve your attitude daily.

- Speak up for what is right.

APPLICATION

Challenge yourself to formulate one unique question. Only one! This question will help you gain a better understanding of your troop. Over the next week, ask. Be mindful of what is said. Expand and inquire further. Remember to listen. Do not interrupt. The next week, come back with the insight you've gained to follow up on what you've discussed. Expand more. Build a deeper connection. Over time, see how that affects your communication with said individual. Apply this tactic with others. Care genuinely.

Chapter

What EVERY NCO Should Know!

"The only true wisdom is in knowing you know nothing."

Socrates

Sure, there are a lot of things an NCO should know. There are a lot of new roles and responsibilities that have now fallen in your lap. Just remember, you aren't alone. We do not have to know everything. Establish bonds and create open forums of communications where you can share and gain knowledge from other NCOs who have gone through what you are going through. Life is all about connection. The Air Force is one big, massive team. One team, one fight! Start looking at it that way. Not everyone is out to get you, I promise. I used to think that everyone was. For nine years, I wasn't a very good team player. I wasn't even on the team. I was watching from the sidelines. It's never too late to turn over a new leaf. We have all failed and made mistakes. No one is perfect. Recognize your failures. Acknowledge them. Make amends. Do not let them hold you back.

NOTHING IS IMPOSSIBLE

Your dreams, visions, and aspirations are all obtainable. The true question is, how committed are you to making them a reality? Are you willing to swim in the deep end and fail? Learn from your mistakes and rise? Anything we set our minds to can be achieved. Do not give up. Create a work environment that supports the fulfillment of dreams and aspirations. Challenge the processes that can be improved. Test new visions. Nothing is impossible.

DON'T FORGET WHERE YOU CAME FROM

Remember we all came in as Airmen. No one was magically enlisted as a SNCO. We all started with humble beginnings or were humbled quite quickly. We went through very challenging obstacles to get to where we are now. Every enlisted member got off that bus at Lackland and spent time at BMT, just like you. They had a similar reason for enlisting. We all had a first assignment. No matter how hard a challenge you face, don't forget where you came from.

PEERS

Lean on your peers in times of struggle. We should be looking out for one another. I'd rather form bonds with brothers and sisters than get paid more any day of the week. The promotion culture has challenged us to rise to the occasion. Bring your peers with you. There is no need to close off a 'peer' just to make a promotion. Gain strength and knowledge from peers. Peers have a diverse spectrum of knowledge, as do you. Learn from your peers and grow with them. Support them. Be there when they need you.

AWARDS AREN'T EVERYTHING

Remind your people that awards are not the things that drive the mission. People are. Sometimes, times and places do not align for individuals to win certain awards. That does not mean their work should not be valued. I've seen a higher level of praise for those award winners, but we must remember, they could never have done those great things without the support of their peers, supervisors, mentors, friends, families, and leaders. It's difficult to watch others continuously win; win at life, win at people, win at you. Your awards will more than likely be forgotten very quickly, for there are four quarters and an annual one with numerous criteria. No one will remember you for how many awards you win. You will be remembered for how you treat people.

GET THE MISSION ACCOMPLISHED

Being too nice is something I have been battling my entire life. I've always looked for ways around 'CCing' people in emails. I'll go out of my way to help when I can to not throw anyone under the bus. What I have learned is, the mission will always get done. It must. There is no choice. However, the way we go about handling people to accomplish it is entirely up to us. Make it fun. Be understanding. You will make mistakes, but learn from them. The mission will always be There. People will not.

BE RELATABLE

Remember the human factor. You may have kids. You may like sports. You may just enjoy life. Do not forget that bringing your true self to work is very important. I remember struggling with the thought of, 'I may have to tone down the jokes when I become an NCO.' For a while, I slowed down, but I realized that was not me. Be relatable. Be you. People appreciate that more than a robot.

HUSTLE

Life isn't fair, nor will it stop for anyone. Awards will always be there! They won't go away. They'll stay on the shelf or wall to collect dust. What are you doing now to create a better Air Force for the next generation? What legacy will you leave behind? How strong is your hustle? The Air Force isn't for you to quit, nor should you be.

FLY, FIGHT, AND WIN

Never forget the bigger picture. Never forget that at any level and any job. You are providing capabilities for mission accomplishment. Your troops may not have a clue as to the fact that what they're doing daily is enabling the bigger picture. Explain exactly why their actions are so important. Break down the mission they are supporting. Give them a reason to do the small tasks. Make them feel important in every task they perform. Ask the fresh eyes what you could be doing better. There are always improvements to be made. People are eager to help if they feel their ideas and performance have deep value.

PLAY THE LONG GAME

"Always work two ranks ahead, mastering the next now."

Jon Burns

Moves shouldn't be made just one step forward. Plan your next five steps. There's written guidance on what to expect for each rank. As promotions go for stratification, looking back two to five years, depending on tier is the Air Force's system. Acquire the promotion system knowledge on force distribution, boards, grading, and promotions to ensure those around you have the highest chance to fulfill their goals. As SNCO boards go, looking back at the last five years of EPRs, you were possibly a SSgt. What are you doing to set yourself up? If this isn't a goal for you, what are you doing to set yourself up for a smooth civilian transition into what you love? Twenty years goes by quickly. What you do now will evolve into results in years to come. Plan and visualize where you would like to be—in life, not just in the Air Force.

LONG GAME PROMOTION FORMULA

As Air force promotion boards go, the last five years of EPRs are evaluated. Keep this in mind while pursuing and working toward your goal.

A1C - SrA - SSgt. As an A1C, you should be mastering the work mindset of a SrA, working toward becoming a SSgt.

SrA - SSgt - TSgt. As a SrA, you should be mastering the work mindset of a SSgt, working toward becoming a TSgt.

SSgt - TSgt - MSgt. As a SSgt, you should be mastering the work mindset of a TSgt, working toward becoming a MSgt.

TSgt - MSgt - SMSgt. As a TSgt, you should be mastering the work mindset of a MSgt, working toward becoming a SMSgt.

MSgt - SMSgt - CMSgt. As a MSgt, you should be mastering the work mindset of a SMSgt, working toward becoming a CMSgt.

As an NCO, you should further your knowledge on certain aspects to make it easier to mentor within each rank. Don't forget, you don't have to know everything. It's all a matter of effort, how you find the resources, who you know, and how you can connect people. The main point I'd like to convey is that as an NCO, you are important. You are valued. You have amazing ideas. You are the most important tier in the Air Force. Directly caring for the Airmen is the first real sight of leadership they get. NCOs have the power to change the climate.

IDEAS

NCOs know what it's like to be an Airman. They have experience. NCOs also know what a true NCO should be like. NCOs have brilliant ideas. Do not let your ideas go unheard. If you feel that your voice isn't valued, keep pursuing your ideas. Chat with multiple people about your ideas. It's bound to gain traction when the time is right. Do not let others bring you down. Once you begin working on an idea, you'll build confidence and flow. Listen to your troops, they also have brilliant ideas. Let the ideas of others be known, and share them. Connect their ideas in the right places, with the right people who will push those ideas into action.

CHANGE

NCOs have seen what an amazing supervisor is. NCOs have seen what a truly poor supervisor is. They have seen both sides of an NCO. NCOs are in a unique place in which they can be the change. Change starts with all of us. You have the choice to make an impact in someone's life each day. Be their change. Go above and beyond. Motivate your Airmen and instill in them the fact that they can accelerate change. They will be our Air Force leaders of tomorrow. We would have never gotten to where we are now without change. Sometimes it's difficult. It takes time. Allow for it. Be patient and consistent. Lead the change.

WHO YOU PORTRAY

An NCO can make or break a career. As an NCO, you're an ambassador of the Air Force culture. The actions and thoughts you portray are a direct reflection of the Air Force. People do not stay at a job because they love the job. They can go somewhere else and do the same job. People stay at their job because they love the people they work with. People do not leave their jobs. People leave their bosses.

CORE VALUES

Our promotion evaluations should be based on our Air Force core values. Practice and apply them daily. I challenge you to find your own unique set of personal core values. They could already be a massive factor in your life. Identify what core values you hold deeply. Further expand them and acknowledge them daily. Remember, no one is perfect. We are still human. Sometimes, you may slip up. Do you habitually slip up, or do you slip up once in a blue moon? Practice, allow these core values to become engrained into the inner workings of your being.

OPPORTUNITIES

If an NCO doesn't know what's going on, how can he pass the information on? Find out what's going on around the wing or group monthly. Compile an email, send it out. Know which individuals are interested in certain opportunities. Push specific information to them directly. It will certainly make them feel important. They will also know that you care. We enlist from all walks of life, people from different backgrounds, with different stories. No two Airmen are alike. But they should all be granted an equal opportunity to thrive in the Air Force. Not only should the opportunity be equal, it should also lead them to excel. An NCO with great vision can lead others to create their own unique vision.

ADVANCEMENT

Knowing when your troop is coming up on a promotion is critical to their success. Lining them up for a promotion is huge. I'm not sure how many times I've briefed based on AFSC data, to find out those Airmen have no idea what the test is comprised of. Most Airmen have no idea that there are two separate tests. One hundred questions on job knowledge, another hundred questions on Air Force knowledge, what those two tests are based on, what study materials are available, promotion statistics throughout the years, or what the EPR point system entails. Going in blind is not how an NCO should prepare their Airmen. Get knowledgeable on our promotion system, including boards, grading, and point systems per EPR rating. The easiest way to do so isn't to just brief. Find the subject matter experts. Inquire and gain knowledge. Write out a briefing with detailed information. Writing out your own briefing will make you think about the process a lot more. You'll also have to find the best data. Present the most unique way. Apply the practices, then teach them.

EPRS

What is a push line? Where do bullets go per section, and why? Is there an order for weakest to strongest bullets? What is the process for getting stratified? Bullets are graded line by line. They account for an entire year's rating. Ask the questions! Change is important. There will come a time when our EPR, grading, and feedback processes will change. Make sure you are on top of the changes and fully learn the difference. The Air Force isn't going to slow down and wait for you to catch up. Your troops will need that information to move their careers forward!

GRADING PACKAGES (EPRS AND AWARDS)

Many NCOs do not have experience when it comes to getting another perspective on writing. Volunteer for this opportunity. You will gain a keen insight into the other side of bullet writing. There is no better learning than gaining more perspective on a subject.

BOARDS

Different squadrons, groups and flights utilize boards for recognition. If the opportunity is there, raise your hand to be on a board. It's an amazing experience offering feedback and learning from those participating on the board. If you have a troop who is going to a board, prep them. Go with them. Coach them. Don't leave them hanging. Walk them through the process. Put them at ease. Boards are nerve-racking. As an NCO, help them find comfort in knowing it's just a board. Literally.

Private Organizations (Booster Club, Top 4, 5/6, Toastmasters, AFSA, etc.)

Don't knock it until you try it. They aren't all 'bullet chasers.' A lot of the NCOs who are members of those organizations are outstanding people and massive contributors to our Air Force community. If you do not have the knowledge, you cannot talk! The perception you give off toward these organizations could hinder a member from wanting to try. Going into the private organizations with a team mindset, and being willing to learn will be beneficial in your success and how you relate it to others. Early on in my career, I was guilty of talking down private organizations. Then I realized, 'Who am I to even talk? What if my troop wants to join an organization and I have no knowledge about it?' My scope of influence would have been lacking. Give it a shot before you speak poorly about it! Go into a private organization for a thirst for knowledge. Forget the bullet. You will gain way more than you expect with the proper mindset. You will come out with more friends and a larger network of peers to start collaborating with. A lot of these organizations give members a distinct purpose, by allowing them the free range to practice and mentor in various ways.

ASSIGNMENT LISTINGS

Our decision to enlist is often based on 'traveling the world.' For your first assignment, you get North Dakota. That can change your outlook on how long you make the Air Force a career. You make that assignment what you want it to be, of course. But giving an Airman the dates and times to apply for overseas assignments, BOP windows, and step-by-step guidance on where to find it all, is crucial to their happiness. I'll never forget the time a friend of mine told me, "I've never changed my assignment preference." My first thought was, 'Yeah, fucking right, you've been in for four years.' Then we head to the computer and walk through the steps to get to the assignment preference section on virtual. I KID YOU NOT, when he pulls it up, the screen reads, 'Welcome to virtual MPF, please enter your information.' The man went four years without a clue of knowing he could PCS! We can do better. You can do better!

MORE THAN A UNIFORM

There will be a day in the future when you take the uniform off for good. You may get the occasional, "Thank you for your service." Not too sure on how retiree benefits apply to military discounts, but hopefully, that 10% off still applies. Civilian employers love our corporate experience because we start at a young age (most of us). What I'm saying is, no one will know or care how many years you've served or what you did in the military. Your grandkids may ask. Now, I'm not saying this isn't an extremely important feat. Be proud. I'm telling you, (insert your name here) is more important. Take care of (insert your name here again). (Insert your name here last for the time) comes first.

Reflection Points

- How are you working toward your plans after the Air Force?
- What could you gain more knowledge about to become a better NCO?

- What unique opportunities can you offer to your people?

- How strong is your hustle? How can you improve it?

Key Takeaways

- It's okay to not know everything, identify people who do.

- Don't forget where you come from.

- Awards are not what people remember, they will remember you.

- Learn from those around you. When support is needed, do not burn your peers. Enlist them for help and support.

- Play the long game. Not everything is going to happen tomorrow.

- Gain multiple perspectives on all topics before making decisions.

APPLICATION

Play the long game. Where do you want to be in five years? What kind of person will you be? What job and character will you have? How will you treat people?

Write down your answer. Explain in detail why those are your answers.

What are your next five steps to get there?

Start moving now!

Chapter

8

Into the Future

"The future is always decided by those who put their imagination to work, who challenge the unknown, and who are not afraid to risk failure."

- General Bernard A. Schriever

Possibilities are endless. Anything is possible. Begin to investigate the future of your personal life and where you envision the Air Force will be in the next ten years. You have all the technology at your disposal. How do you choose to use it? How do you choose to apply it in your work sections? How can you integrate civilian partners in your field of work now? The action and innovation you put in place now will lead to results ten years from now. Start getting to work! As an NCO influencer, keep your people in the know of what is going on. The current and upcoming challenges you will face are unknown until you seek the answers. Where do you see the Air Force ten years from now? What actions can you take to leave it better than you found it?

VISION OF THE FORCE

Here's my vision of how we can change the Force. Now, this is my opinion—just an idea. After reading, I'd like you to take some time to really think about the beginning workings of the Air Force and what changes can be made from the lowest to highest level. BMT was structured for ground warfare. MTIs are overstressed, and this, in turn, leads to trainees becoming extremely stressed. Now, I am not saying it isn't beneficial, but can this be changed to a more relaxed and constructive environment for learning? At BMT, I would identify strengths and unique competencies before those members move on to their tech schools. Once those competencies are identified, those Airmen would be trained (broken out into their groups), to further expand their knowledge. Their primary AFSC would remain the same, but an additional number or letter would be added to the back end to recognize what that individual specializes in, such as data analytics, programming, arts, leadership, engineering, etc. The possibility here is endless. We often notice Airmen to NCOs years down the line, with incredible resources that were never identified or utilized. This leads me to the topic of multifaceted Airmen.

MULTIFACETED AIRMEN

The Air Force gives us as NCOs a sense of entitlement, which is extremely wrong. Some people think that since we're an NCO, we must no longer do the day-to-day tasks like manning the gate, taking out the trash, putting the reports in; all those simple tasks. We're wrong for thinking that. We can, and should, help in all areas that we can. We should be learning new ways to enhance operations for everyone. What if the Air Force trained people in a more diverse way? What if we could learn two to three AFSCs and bounce around when manning was appropriate and needed? We could bring back some serious knowledge to our work centers, especially if every primary AFSC we worked with had a diverse secondary.

INNOVATION

Diversity of approach + shared goal = Innovation

Enlisting a team of members who all share the same common vision of innovation is crucial. When the team tries different approaches toward that common vision, innovation arises. I challenge you to look for diverse teams. Look at the broken programs and processes in your area. As a team, come up with different ways to innovate. Set the tone for innovation for years to come in your section. Be the culture the Air Force needs. As an NCO, you can do it!

ADDITIONAL RESOURCES

The Air Force follows the corporate model. The Air Force is a corporation of many employees. With such vast numbers, more factors are needed to create a balance. Human resources. Another idea I've had for a while is to add life coaches, process improvement specialists, and other subject matter experts into each squadron. The coaches could give **real** feedback to those who need it, coaching them toward the best personal direction that seems fit. A process improvement specialist could look around the workplace and address what needs to be fixed. Sure, it happens when inspections take place, but what if they were all prevented prior to this? Not only prevented, but totally transformed into a new and better system with the efforts of everyone working together.

Reflection Points

- What changes would you make in the Air Force if you had a magic wand?

- Where do you see the Air Force in ten years?

- What could you implement now to enhance operations directly in your work center?

- What tools can you offer to help your troops to implement what they're passionate about?

Takeaways

- Look to the future.

- Leave it better than you found it.

- Influence innovation.

- Form teams to create ideas and work together.

- Identify those around you with unique competencies.

- Integrate technology and partner with the civilian sector when possible.

APPLICATION

Take the time to research where the Air Force is heading. Check out local businesses in your community that are similar to what you do at work. Seek mentoring and knowledge there. Try to build a partnership. Share that understanding and resource with those around you. Challenge them to find out more and continue building those networking channels.

Book Suggestions

- *Man's Search for Meaning* by Viktor E. Frankl.

- *The 7 Habits of Highly Effective People* by Stephen Covey.
- *Attitude is Everything* by Jeff Keller.
- *Atomic Habits* by James Clear.
- *I Hear You* by Michael Sorenson.
- *Wooden on Leadership* by John Wooden & Steve Jamison.
- *The 12 Week Year* by Brian Moran & Michael Lennington.
- *Staring Down the Wolf* by Mark Divine.
- *Your Next Five Moves* by Patrick Bet-David.
- *Limitless* by Jim Kwik.
- *The Servant* by James Hunter.
- *The Four Agreements* by Don Miguel Ruiz.
- *How To Win Friends & Influence People* by Dale Carnegie.
- *The 21 Irrefutable Law of Leadership* by John Maxwell.
- *S.S.G.T* by CMSgt (Ret) Bob Vasquez.
- *So Ya Wanna Be THE Chief?* by CMSgt (Ret) Bob Vasquez.

CLOSING THOUGHTS

The NCO who inspired my outlook is no longer serving in the Air Force. Recently separated, we still communicate just as we did almost three years ago. From learning about this book, he has been inspired to write his own. It goes both ways. People and connections are a beautiful thing. Brothers, sisters… Build those bonds. They will last forever.

It sounds crazy, I know. The reason for writing this book was simple. To connect and influence NCOs to work toward their goals. This was also a reach to find more likeminded NCOs. There's no stopping what we can do together. Thank you for taking the time out of your life to read this book. If you have any suggestions, additions, things you enjoyed, if you're seeking a mentor, or just in need of someone to chat with, hit my line anytime.

There is one thing I need you to keep in mind. Reading this book may have, hopefully, expanded your thoughts and potential of where you can go. Let me tell you, nothing can come into effect without initiative and application. Start working and grinding in the area you love. No one can stop you but yourself. Get out of your head and into your life. What are your goals and dreams? What change in our culture will you make? I'm looking forward to hearing all about it! The Tongue and Quill can't knock me on this signature block format! Also, excuse the medical group's weird new email. Sincerely, I look forward to hearing from you!

Your friend

Harrison Burkardt

harrison.e.burkardt.mil@mail.mil

Acknowledgments

Jayden – For teaching me that life isn't always a rush and teaching me to enjoy the small things. For accepting me for who I am, understanding my failures, loving me through the difficult times, allowing me time to grow, and growing together. You've shown me that love is effort; a continuous choice.

Leana – For teaching me how to be myself fully and practicing the art of laughter. After your death, I lived in a cloud for countless years, never accepting that I needed help. Thank you for teaching me that I must come first to ensure that others can come after.

Leon – For reminding me daily to treat everyone with love and kindness. Your head will always be the biggest on the planet. Mr. Bighead, stop growing that brain!

Edison – For showing me the fun in everything. You'll always be a monkey's uncle.

Indigo – For reminding me that there is innocence in everyone.

My Dad – For teaching me to always do things right. People are why we are here on Earth, to connect and share it with.

My Mom – For teaching me not to let people walk over me, to take the initiative and go after what is right, even when others may look at me sideways.

Brison – For giving me my wings and allowing me to fly. You've shown me that memories last, small or big.

Ben – For being you and allowing me to always be me. Truly, you've shown me that there isn't anything a friendship can't handle.

Dan – For being a brother from another mother. You've shown me that friendship can withstand the test of time.

Lucas – For listening. Your perspective is kind. You're always looking at both sides. You never judge. You're always walking in someone else's shoes.

Rick – For teaching me that people can connect in a short time. Your care for people is unmatched. Every conversation we have opens my mind! You're the true example of 2000s era 'promote now.'

Ellsworth AFB Dental Leadership Circa 2010-2015 – For showing me that NCOs are humans who care, and that people always come first.

Davis Monthan AFB personnel circa 2016-2020 – For showing me that I made constant excuses and blamed others for my unhappiness. For helping me find my true self.

SMSgt "Hiz" – For showing me that people are genuine and that all it takes is validation. Over the past few months, you've taught me perspective and transparency.

MSgt Ogle – For showing me it doesn't take getting to know someone to care. Just caring makes the difference. I'm grateful for your knowledge and constant advice.

TSgt Boone – For teaching me that Jesus' slippers really do prevent foot fungi. Kidding! For teaching me that humor is a special gift and not to take everything so seriously. The world needs more laughter.

TSgt Howell – For being you! You genuinely care about people. You've shown me to be my full self, whether at work or not. Thank you for always being you!

MSgt Jones – For teaching me that there are probably three thousand of you in the Air Force! For teaching me to invite others, build a team, and let others learn and be involved.

CMSgt Vasquez – For believing in me. For pushing me to continue writing and all your help on becoming a successful NCO! Heirpower!

Davis Monthan Honor Guard – For showing me what a true military 'family' is.

All the Airmen I've had the pleasure of talking to regarding leadership – You teach me daily that we can never stand still. There's always more to learn and grow. I look forward to seeing where you'll be in ten years from now!

My circle – For teaching me to keep it real and not to settle for complacency. I've learned how important it is to push and grind until you reach your passion in life.

You – For supporting me and reading this book!